# Memories
## of
# Wrexham

*True North Books Ltd*

# Memories
## of
# Wrexham

Wrexham Farmers' Union.
WREXHAM FARMERS'
CHARITY SALE
to be held at this SMITHFIELD
1 p.m. to-day.
All kinds of PRODUCE.
Calves, Sheep, Lambs, Pigs, Garden
Plants, Cheese, Butter, Eggs,
Poultry (dressed and alive).
All the above to be sold by Auction.
Proceeds will be given to Local
Hospitals.
DON'T FORGET 1 O'CLOCK TO-DAY

The Publishers would like to thank the following
companies for supporting the production of this book

Air Products UK Limited

Allington Hughes Solicitors

Flexsys

Fort James (UK) Limited

Kent Supplies (Wrexham) Limited

Kronospan Limited

Rexam (part of Rexam plc's Coated films and Papers sector)

Royalite Industrial Sheet

Dennis Ruabon Limited

TACP

Thomas Transport (Wrexham) Limited

JH Willis Limited

First published in Great Britain by True North Books Limited
England HX5 9AE

ISBN 1 900463 23 7

Text, design and origination by True North Books Limited
Printed and bound by The Amadeus Press Limited

# Memories are made of this

**M**emories. We all have them; some good, some bad, but our memories of the town we grew up in are usually tucked away in a very special place in our minds. The best are usually connected with our childhood and youth, when we longed to be grown up and paid no attention to adults who told us to enjoy our youth, as these were the best years of our lives. We look back now and realise that they were right.

We remember crowding into the Saturday morning matinee at the Odeon

with our mates to throw bits of rubbish around and watch the cliffhanger serial that left its heroine, pale-faced but still beautiful, tied to the railway line for a whole nailbiting week. And we remember the hot Vimto we bought from the herbalist in Bridge Street; congregating at Sam's Ice Cream Parlour in Chester Road or at the Milk Bar in Hope Street. We recall dancing the night away at St Mary's church hall, and our very first pint at The Horns - or was it the Seven Stars?

So many memories. And so many changes. Wrexham in the 1950s, when the trading estate was developed on the site of what had been during the war the Royal Ordnance Factory at Marchwiel, attracting large companies and new industries to Wrexham and providing thousands of new jobs. What a difference it made to the town!

And we can think of sweeping changes of a different kind, when those first self-serve stores opened in the 1960s. Remember when the Majestic became Coopers supermarket? And the days when Tesco had a store in High Street? How strange it felt at first to help ourselves from the goods on display on the shelves - it was almost like stealing!

Through the bad times and the good, however, Wrexham not only survived but prospered. We have only to compare the town as it is today with its new shopping centres and up-to-the-minute facilities with the town as it was, say in the 1940s, to see what progress has been realised and what achievements have been made over the last 50 years. Wrexham has a history to be proud of - but more importantly, a great future to look forward to, into the new millennium and beyond.

# Contents

# Around the town centre

A photograph to stir many memories, showing the Hand Inn and the old Town Hall before their demolition. An earlier inn of the same name, built in the early 18th century, once occupied the site of the Hand Inn, though it was known by a number of other names until around 1800. Amazingly, the carved beams on the front of the old inn dated from the 16th century; whatever happened to those historic old beams when the old Hand Inn was demolished in 1899? A 1940s road widening scheme saw the end of the inn's successor, along with the old Town Hall. On the far right, Dodmans shoe shop were advertising 'Xmas Gifts', which dates the picture as having been taken in December, though the year is unfortunately unknown. One of the oldest in Wrexham, this shop still survives today and is greatly valued locally for its genuine atmosphere and character. The blinds are still down in some of the shops, and there was no traffic in the street to disturb the peace. There are a number of people about, however - though they don't appear to be going anywhere. Perhaps they were employees in the local shops, waiting for the boss to turn up with a key so that they could start their working day?

> THE CARVED BEAMS ON THE FRONT OF THE ORIGINAL HAND INN DATED FROM THE SIXTEENTH CENTURY

The partly obscured signs in this photograph, taken before the road widening scheme that changed the view for ever, allow us to confidently identify this as having been taken during the second world war, when place names and other identifying marks were painted out to confuse the enemy about exactly where they were. Dorrofield's tobacconist and confectioners on the far left of the photograph were advertising Capstan cigarettes; this was in the days before the effects of smoking on health were recognised and advertising discontinued. The baby shop next door was the rather distinguished-sounding Madam Jobyns;

Rees's drapers shop on the corner of Town Hill was boarded up. The old Town Hall opposite housed the wholesale and retail wines and spirits business of Thomas Williams & Co. Across Church Street are the solid and reassuring walls of the Westminster Bank, later the TSB. Today the building still stands, though its banking facilities have long gone. Recent proposals have included turning it into a wine bar; watch this space.

Note the unattended cycle leaning against the post box. In those rather more honest days you could hope to find your bike still there when you returned to it!

**Above:** Wrexham's traffic problems were few back in the 1930s as we can see from the mere handful of vehicles in Brook Street. There was a steeper than normal camber on part of this stretch of road, and the houses further along are noticeably lower than the pavement. The reason for this lay in the fact that the River Gwenfro ran underneath Brook Street, which was culverted. A number of men, women and children have clustered together at the entrance to the arched passageway through the terrace of houses; perhaps they lived in Brook Square, which lay to the rear of Brook Street. Bedrooms above the archway would have provided a little more living space for the families fortunate enough to have secured one of these houses. The old British School can be seen the background, and the factory with the tall chimney in the background was the premises of L Rowlands Ltd, who used the building as a wholesale depot for their pharmaceuticals business. As the traditional coal, brewing, steel and leather industries declined, particularly in the post-war years, the chemicals industry was one that grew up, along with other modern industries such as electronic products, to replace them.

**Right:** The Wynnstay Arms Hotel faces us in this view of High Street, possibly taken during the 1930s. M R Evans tobacconist on the left advertises Gold Flake; the link between cigarettes and cancer had not been recognised at that time. Is it a case of 'false memory syndrome' - or did nearly everybody smoke back then? It was to be a further 40 years or so before advertisers would enter into a voluntary agreement with the Department of Health to declare the dangers connected with cigarette smoking, and 'Cigarettes can seriously damage your health' appeared at the foot of adverts. W Phillips & Co, next door to Evans', were a popular Wrexham grocer. The North and South Wales Bank can be seen on the left in the distance; they were taken over by the Midland Bank in 1908. The Wynnstay Arms has an interesting history. Earmarked for demolition, the townspeople not surprisingly opposed the redevelopment of the ancient hostelry, which at one time boasted a special bus which transported hotel guests to and from the railway station. In the end, however, a compromise was reached; the building's original facade was preserved while a brand new hotel was built behind it.

A view of Queen Street that has now vanished for ever. We do not have an exact date for this photograph, though it probably dates from around 1960. Perhaps it was taken at the end of the working day when people were on their way home: the confectioner has clearly had a successful day - the display shelves in the window are virtually empty, and the blinds are down in Ernest Busfield's.

The 1960s saw the rapid rise to popularity of the foreign holiday, and the Denbighshire Travel Agent on the left is advertising travel by land, sea and air. Many first-time travellers to destinations such as Austria or Italy chose to go by rail rather

than to fly; holiday brochures usually offered either option.

When plans for redevelopment of the area were first put forward, the intention was to keep the arched entrance to the vegetable market and these rather attractive Tudor-style frontages on the corner of Lambpit Street (though the building was not as old as it would appear to have been at first glance). Readers may remember however, that the building stood empty for such a long time that the vagaries of the British weather put paid to any hopes of saving it, and eventually the bulldozers moved in. The Henblas Square shopping development was eventually built there.

**Below:** Though this scene in Pentrefelin Road was captured on camera in January 1956, Humphreys Woodworkers were still advertising their speciality - making and repairing mangle rollers. For the benefit of younger readers who have grown up with automatic washing machines and tumble dryers, a mangle was to their grandmothers an indispensable part of washday equipment. The housewife (yes, never the men!) would squeeze the water out of wet washing between a pair of heavy wooden rollers - and winding the handle that turned the rollers was hard work. By the 1950s more families could afford to buy electric washing machines. Some electric machines still had small rubber rollers and a handle; the de luxe kind had electrically-operated rollers. Humphreys were still operating their repair service in the mid-1950s, though the days of the old-fashioned mangle were definitely numbered.

The Mitre Inn, selling Border ales, was still open, though many of the surrounding streets had already been demolished, no doubt affecting their trade. The 'Free Car Park' (oh for the same facility today!) was once Hughes Court. The photograph, looking north-west from Brook Street, will no doubt stir many memories that will include the quiet purr of mangle rollers being turned. Can't you just hear them now!

*Regent Street around 1960, when the Imperial Hotel still stood on the corner of King Street. It was later to be demolished as part of the town centre redevelopment programme, and the Job Centre now stands on the site. And do you remember the Majestic Cinema? In the early years of the 20th century the building was a roller skating rink; it opened as The Rink cinema in May, 1911. It soon became the Majestic, however, and was to remain so for many years. With an amazing 1800 seats, the Majestic had the privilege of being recognised as the largest cinema in North Wales. In the 1930s and 40s, the heyday of the cinema, a seat in the art-deco style Majestic cost as little as fourpence - though the better off could pay a shilling for a superior seat. Today the flamboyant Elihu Yale Wine Bar, the establishment attracts a young clientèle. Nearby the exciting new Regent Street retail development draws in shoppers from a wide area, with a selection of shops, stores and services to suit everyone. While the shopping centre caters for Wrexham's physical needs, the Methodist Church upstairs caters for the spiritual - along with the many other churches and chapels in the town.*

Wouldn't it be nice to know what all these people were waiting for? Could it be that this was the old Town Hall's last day and that the bulldozers are about to move in on the doomed building? Certainly there are many posters displayed on the doors and walls. The presence of the law tells us that something was about to happen - and whatever it was, these men and children are determined to watch.

The Town Hall was built early in the 18th century and took the place of the ancient Shirehall building, which in the mid 16th century stood on

or very near to the site. When it was first constructed the building was very different; the ground floor was an open space which housed the town's market, while the room upstairs was used as a courtroom. Walls were eventually built to enclose the structure. Thomas Williams & Co ran a wines and spirits business on the ground floor, as the wonderful frieze that ran around the building informs us: Thos Williams & Co Wrexham Ltd, Proprietors of His Majesty's Bonded Stores. The adjoining Burtons building advertises that the billiard hall is to let.

## A trip through the 1930s

**WHAT'S ON..?**
*In this heyday of the cinema, horrified audiences were left gasping at the sight of Fay Wray in the clutches of the giant ape in the film 'King Kong', released in 1933. Very different but just as gripping was the gutsy 1939 American Civil War romance 'Gone with the Wind'. Gable's parting words, 'Frankly, my dear, I don't give a damn' went down in history.*

**GETTING AROUND...**
*At the beginning of the decade many believed that the airship was the transport of the future. The R101 airship, however, loaded with thousands of cubic metres of hydrogen, crashed in France on its maiden flight in 1930. Forty-eight passengers and crew lost their lives. In 1937 the Hindenburg burst into flames - the entire disaster caught on camera and described by a distraught reporter. The days of the airship were numbered.*

**SPORTING CHANCE...**
*The black American Jesse Owens won a brilliant four world records in the 1936 Olympic Games in Berlin, thumbing the nose to Adolph Hitler's dreams of Aryan superiority. In a petty display Hitler walked out of the stadium and 'took his bat home'; later he refused to have his photograph taken with the victorious Owens.*

**Above:** Apart from losing a few of these tall and shady trees, Rhosddu Road has not changed all that much since 1953, when this photograph was taken. The date was May, and although a couple of people are sitting in the hazy sunshine we can judge by the coats and scarves worn by a number of passers-by that the weather was not particularly warm that day. A convenient form of head covering that could be simply folded up and popped into a handbag, headscarves were fashionable during the 1940s and 50s. The lady in the photograph was in good company - Her Majesty the Queen was herself a great wearer of headscarves. Looking towards Argyle Street, note the sign on the left advertising Prices Domestic Registry. Whether you wanted a job as a parlourmaid or a cook general, or were seeking a domestic servant of any kind, this domestic employment agency was the place to go. These buildings have now been replaced by modern shops, and indeed not too far away from this spot Wrexham was to see enormous changes a few years on when the new Guild Hall would be built on the site of the old vicarage.

**Right:** Doesn't it seem strange to see open fields around Wrexham where the large modern shopping complex stands today? Sainsburys supermarket and filling station now occupy a large proportion of this land, and along with the many other shops and stores on the site offer a huge shopping choice with free car parking to local people. The multi-screen Odeon Cinema opened in 1998. A visit to 'the pictures' was a popular pastime until the late 1950s, when television ousted the cinema as a leisure activity, and many cinemas went on to become Bingo halls. Cinema-going remained unpopular until recent years, when the tide turned once more, and out of town multi-screen cinemas are today mushrooming around towns and cities across Wales and England. In the centre of the photograph, the Technical College was still being built. The architects gained a Royal Institute of British Architects bronze medal and diploma as the best building constructed in the Liverpool Architectural Society's area between 1951-53 - and took pride in being the first building in Wales to achieve this status. The large national construction firm Holland & Hannen and Cubitts Ltd undertook the construction of the new college.

**Left:** This part of Wrexham has undergone such vast changes that it is virtually unrecognisable as the same area today. Shot in 1952 during the building of the Technical College, this aerial photograph shows not only the development of the complex of college buildings but serves as a record of the past history of the town. Just creeping into the edge of the picture is the grounds of the Wrexham Football Club, while across the road is the estate of prefabs that were built to cope with an increasing need for housing. Partly concealed in the wooded area further to the right along Mold Road is the Maes Gwyn Masonic Hall, well known even at the time for its fine facilities. Nearby readers will pick out the rooftops of the Crosville bus depot, and the rows of buses standing in the yard behind.

An interesting point is the almost total lack of private cars in this photograph, both on the estates and on the main roads, which appeared to be little more than country lanes in the early 1950s. At that time Britain still had a long way to go before post-war prosperity became a reality, and a car was an unattainable dream for the average family.

**Below:** Construction of the Denbigh Technical College was well underway when this photograph was taken on 24th November 1951, and the leafless trees give a forlorn wintry air to the chilly scene. The college that emerged at the end of it, however, was worth waiting for and was a facility that Wrexham could be proud of. The half-finished building and its muddy grounds and rough tracks pictured here bear no resemblance to the clean lines of the finished college buildings that were officially opened by the Duchess of Gloucester almost exactly two years later. The exciting air of change and development in the town continues today, and Mold Road, in the background of the photograph, is to undergo a £1 million landscaping and facelift in the near future.

On the left in the background is the Wrexham Football Club, its walls usefully employed in advertising the Wrexham Motor Company and the Wrexham Dairies. Between the stadium and the college are Nissen huts erected during World War II, which were later taken over by squatters, whose washing can be seen blowing on the line. On the skyline is the spire of St Mary's Roman Catholic pro cathedral, and near the trees towards the right readers might just pick out the hospital's water tower.

The Parish Church clock records that it was almost lunch time, and Hope Street, always one of the busiest shopping streets in Wrexham, was particularly so in this 1960s view, probably taken one Saturday morning. Shoppers then shared the street with moving traffic and tightly-parked cars, and the wonderful old vehicles range from the Morris Minor to the mini that was beloved by so many motorists of the day. Pedestrianisation has made shopping so much simpler and safer, and today parents can shop without worrying that their child might suddenly dart in front of a car. The shops and services in Hope Street will ring many a nostalgic bell: the Maypole Dairy was on the left, as was Paige ladies' fashion shop and Francis & Co Chemists. The National Provincial Bank was next door to Woolworths - always a favourite port of call with its competitive prices. Duttons' Sig Ar Ro grocer's shop was on the corner of High Street. Across the road was Burton's menswear, the Littlewoods store, Melias grocers, a well-known name in the town, and Briggs' shoe shop. Marks & Spencer just off the picture on the far right was already earmarked for extension.

This fascinating view of the Town Hill and Brook Street area of Wrexham dates back to the early 1960s. Left of centre is the Drill Hall in Chapel Street, with its gable end facing on to the field. A place that has seen much action over the years, the Wrexham Home Guard trained there during the second world war. Sharp eyes might pick out the back of the Kings Arms pub in Bridge Street, originally The Horns. The railway line bisects the top portion of the photograph; closed now to the railway network the line was utilised for St Giles Way. Opened in 1998, Wrexham can be justifiably proud of the new link road for which the town waited 36 years! The parish church of St Giles itself can be seen in the top right corner. Below the railway line is the Albion car park (the site of the old Albion Brewery) and the old toilet block - another area which has changed for the better with the recent building of brand new loos.

The almost triangular site on the right was once the home of the Eagle Foundry in Tuttle Street, where Cudworth and Johnson went down in history as the first firm in Wrexham to install telephones. The building in the lower right corner is St Giles School.

## A trip through the 1940s

**WHAT'S ON?**
In wartime Britain few families were without a wireless set. It was the most popular form of entertainment, and programmes such as ITMA, Music While You Work and Mrs Dale's Diary provided the people with an escape from the harsh realities of bombing raids and ration books. In 1946 the BBC introduced the Light Programme, the Home Service and the Third Programme, which gave audiences a wider choice of listening.

**GETTING AROUND**
October 1948 saw the production of Britain's first new car designs since before the war. The Morris Minor was destined for fame as one of the most popular family cars, while the four-wheel-drive Land Rover answered the need for a British-made off-road vehicle.
The country was deeply in the red, however, because of overseas debts incurred during the war. The post-war export drive that followed meant that British drivers had a long wait for their own new car.

**SPORTING CHANCE**
American World Heavyweight Boxing Champion Joe Louis, who first took the title back in 1937, ruled the world of boxing during the 1930s and 40s, making a name for himself as unbeatable. Time after time he successfully defended his title against all comers, finally retiring in 1948 after fighting an amazing 25 title bouts throughout his boxing career. Louis died in 1981 at the age of 67.

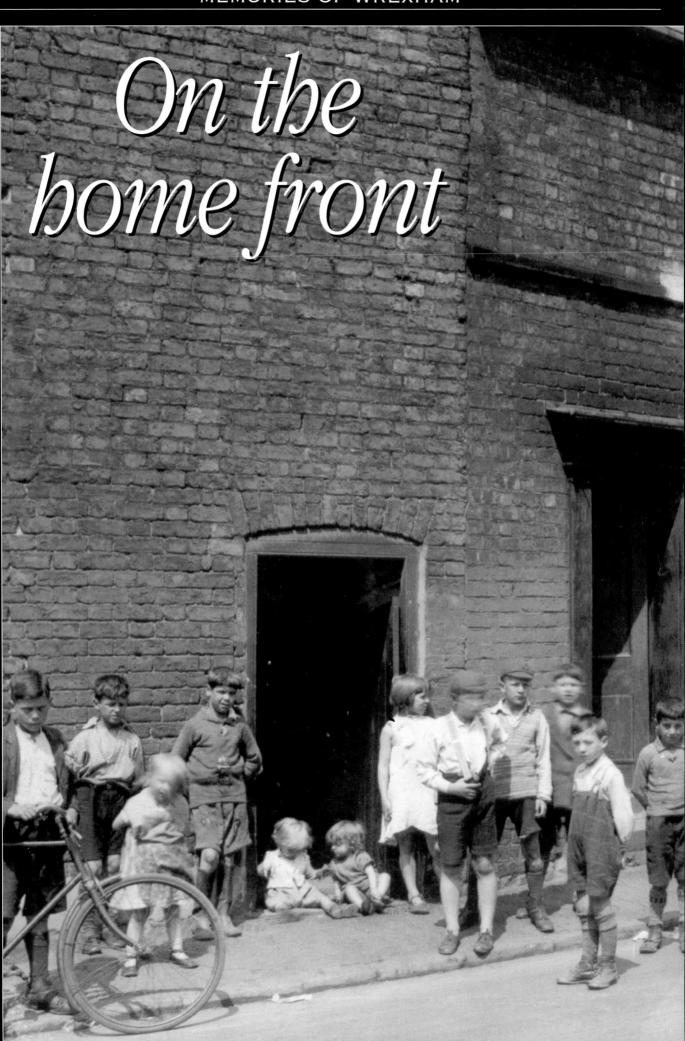

# *On the home front*

One area of Wrexham that changed beyond all recognition was Farndon Street, Kendrick Place, and the surrounding streets of tightly-packed terrace houses. Though the families who lived here may not have had much in the way of material possessions there would nevertheless have been a very strong feeling of community. It was safer then to allow children to play outside, and the streets and back yards became a playground for the many children living there. It may be that some readers who spent their childhood there will remember those days with fondness; there was little money to spend on toys (the little boy who owned a bike (left) would have been in the minority) but at least they had plenty of playmates. Those wonderful games of tig, tin can squat, whip and top, marbles, and perhaps shuttlecock and battledore. What a contrast with the children of today, who have their own computers and scores of computer games, televisions in their bedrooms, the latest 'in' toys and even perhaps their own mobile phone - yet whose cry is so often 'I'm bored!' Imprisoned by a society who dare not let their children wander the streets, today's 'privileged' children are often isolated in an indoor world with few friends to play with. The date of the photographs has been forgotten, but these scenes are from the 1930s. The open windows indicate that this was a warm day, yet even so many caps and hats are in evidence here, even among the children. Hats were an accepted part of the day's fashion and men, women and children alike would rarely have been seen in public without some kind of headgear. The older gentleman posing with the children for the photograph (left) is wearing the full ensemble of waistcoat, jacket and hat. With Holt Street in the distance, Farndon Street was destined to become part of the Do-it-All car park (later Tesco's).

A bunch of children and a couple of their mums have grouped together and smile cheerfully for the camera (above) while other residents stand in the doorways of their houses - numbers one to five, Harrison's Court. We have no date for either picture - but a little detective work leads us to deduce that they were not taken on a Monday. The washing lines that stretch across the yard were empty, which they would surely not have been had it been Monday, the traditional washing day! Why and where the tradition was established we do not know, but probably for centuries Monday remained wash day right up until the coming of automatic washing machines and the practice of more women going out to work.

There were a number of men about at the time these photographs were taken, so perhaps the photographer called round one Saturday morning. Wrexham had a number of industries at the time, and the men would perhaps work in the breweries or the brickworks, or they would work in the leather tanning industry or in steel production. A number of them would possibly work as miners; at one time coal was a major industry in Wrexham with as many as 36 pits operating in the area. Always a hazardous occupation, a mining disaster at the Gresford Colliery tragically claimed 265 lives on 22nd September 1934. The tragedy was one of the worst mining accidents in Britain. Industry was to decline in Wrexham after the second world war; the tanneries closed down, as did the brickworks, and when the coal reserves began to run out the mines closed one by one. Bersham, Wrexham's last colliery, closed down in 1988. Harrison's Court, situated behind Farndon Street, was scheduled for demolition and these families would soon find themselves uprooted from their tight-knit community.

# A TRIP THROUGH THE 1950s

## WHAT'S ON?

Television hit Britain in a big way during the 1950s. Older readers will surely remember 'Double Your Money', 'Dixon of Dock Green' and 'Dragnet' (whose characters' names were changed 'to protect the innocent').

Commercial television was introduced on 22nd September 1955, and Gibbs SR toothpaste were drawn out of the hat to become the first advert to be shown. Many believed adverts to be vulgar, however, and audiences were far less than had been hoped for.

## GETTING AROUND

The year 1959 saw the development of the world's first practical air-cushion vehicle - better known to us as the hovercraft. The earliest model was only able to travel at slow speeds over very calm water and was unable to carry more than three passengers. The faster and smoother alternative to the sea ferry quickly caught on, and by the 1970s a 170-ton car-carrying hovercraft service had been introduced across the English Channel.

## SPORTING CHANCE

The four-minute mile had remained the record since 1945, and had become regarded as virtually unbreakable. On 6th May 1954, however, Oxford University student Roger Bannister literally ran away with the record, accomplishing the seemingly impossible in three minutes 59.4 seconds. Bannister collapsed at the end of his last amazing lap, even temporarily losing his vision. By the end of the day, however, he had recovered sufficiently to celebrate his achievement in a London night club!

*Note the number of local residents who came out of doors to pose for the photographer; we should remember that sixty or so years ago far fewer people owned cameras, and having a photograph taken was still quite a rare and special event. An interesting feature of this view is the way these residents' living space overflowed into the yard; mangles, dolly tubs, buckets and tables were a standard feature. And note the wonderful old hip bath - and the bucket to fill it with - hanging on the wall outside one of the houses. Living space was very limited, of course, inside these small cottages, so the family's weekly wash had to be done outside. And not only the family wash; women rarely went out to work at that time so many of them took in washing from the more affluent people in the town. Coping with rain, hail, sleet, snow and all the other aspects of the British weather was all part of the job for these women. Every washday these lines would have been filled with clothes drying in the wind. Brook Street, Brook Square, Farndon Street, Harrison's Court - all were in the Borough of Wrexham's clearance area, and were marked for demolition. One hopes that these families about to be rehoused were happy in their new homes and that their sense of community would be re-established in a different area of the town.*

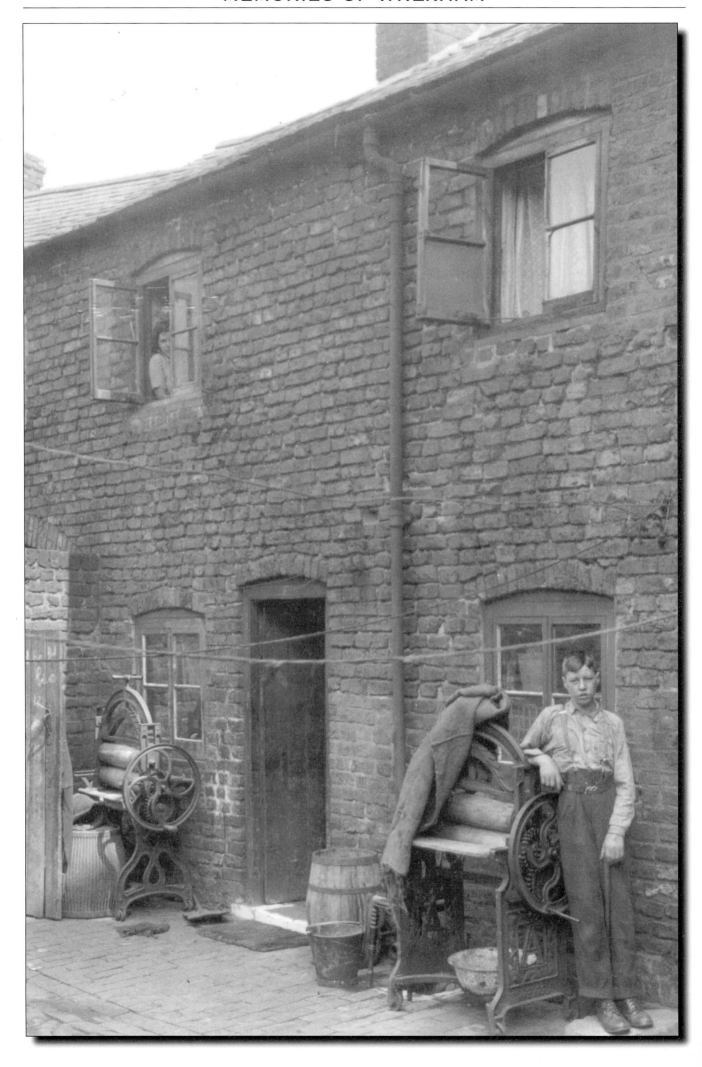

**Left:** Brook Square, and a young teenager nonchalantly leans against the mangle for this photograph while a girl takes in the scene from an upper window. Children have been chalking on the wooden door into the yard - was the perpetrator this young lad or one of his brothers or sisters? Over the years, Wrexham's clearance plans have increased the number of council houses available to families, and also the number of new houses built for sale. In the 1930s a deposit of around £27 with repayments in the region of 14/- a week would have secured you one of these brand new homes. The full price would have been about £500. This entire area is unrecognisable today; when these particular industrial terraces between the British School and Bridge Street were cleared, the site was used for the building of the Odeon cinema (today a Top Rank Bingo hall). Farndon Street, Harrison's Court and Brown Horse Yard also disappeared and eventually rows of new shops, a multi-storey car park, a new Chinese restaurant and the Do-it-All store (now the Aldi supermarket) were built on nearby sites. The large Tesco store was built where Kenyon Street and Kendrick Place used to be.

**Above:** The Old British School (which was no longer operating as a school at the time this photograph was taken) rather forbiddingly overshadows the end of Brook Square, giving the old street a rather claustrophobic atmosphere. The school was built in the 1840s on the site of an old tan yard; the site was donated by an unusually forward-thinking Wrexham citizen, Mr A W Thornley, who was concerned about the lack of education provided for the poorer classes. Education of the labouring classes was an unpopular subject with many Victorian employers who believed that education led to unrest. The British School was built, however, and was not only attended by children but also by adults who wanted to be better informed. Brook Square, which adjoined the school, became widely known as Mary Ann Square - a tribute to their benefactor Mr Thornley's wife, Mary Ann. The school closed in 1901, which must have been a sad day for its last headmaster Charles Dodd. The facility was transferred to Victoria School in Poyser Street. The photograph reveals that Brook Square was home to many families; they were a community and this was their normal environment - and the neighbours standing in their doorways, and the group of children playing in the street seem contented enough with their surroundings. This was 1933, however, and their whole familiar area was about to be erased for ever from the Wrexham street plan.

> IN THE 1930S A DEPOSIT OF £27 WOULD HAVE SECURED YOU A BRAND NEW HOME

**Left: A** broken chair, an old table, galvanised tin baths and tubs, buckets and mangles - all were essential to the way of life in Brook Street in the 1930s. Bathrooms, of course, had long been an undreamed-of luxury to the families who lived in the community, and keeping a large family clean meant a great deal of hard work for every long-suffering mother. Once a week she would have set up a galvanised tin bath (such as the one hanging on this outside wall) in the kitchen, and painstakingly filled it with hot water by way of a bucket. One tub of hot water would probably be all that was available for the entire family. Toilets, usually marked with house numbers for identification , were situated in the yard and were often shared by more than one family. The lives of these residents, however, were soon to take a turn for the better. Their homes were scheduled for demolition, and rehousing would no doubt provide them with the once unimagined joys of a bathroom with hot running water and an indoor toilet, and a tiled kitchen with modern conveniences.

**Below:** Three smart lads pose for the camera in this picture from the late 1950s, bringing memories of our school days flooding back. The first thing to strike us is just how smart the little lads were, despite the fact that money was tight and it was not always easy to find cash to spend on clothing. Still, people did the best with what they had, homemade haircuts and hand-me-down clothes made up for the lack of money when the need arose. The picture highlights just how much fashions have changed since the era featured here. Try getting your little lad to wear short trousers and white ankle socks... let alone a tie!

A nostalgic glimpse backwards at a part of Wrexham that no longer exists *(Inset)* - along the ridge tiles of a line of outside toilets in Ashfield Road. The 1950s were years when many ordinary families began to feel the effects of post-war prosperity that had been looked-for since 1945.

The photograph shows an interesting mixture of old and new; though some of these homes sported television aerials, they still lacked the facility of a modern bathroom. Tin baths were still the order of the day for the inhabitants of these houses, though the washing hanging on the line might well have been done with the aid of a modern electric washing machine.

With their own yard to the rear of the house, the people who lived here would have been luckier than some who lived in the town a decade or two earlier, whose homes faced straight on to the pavement or into a shared courtyard.

These terraces in Ashfield Road were eventually demolished and in the 1960s were replaced by rows of modern houses *(main picture)*. Families who occupy these homes today will be interested to see them in the process of construction; while one man is busy with a pick in the background, another confers with the overseer (or is this the building inspector?). Others are busy in the foreground, sawing piles of timber to the correct lengths. Enormous tins of paint wait for the interiors of the new houses to be ready for those important finishing touches. It would have been an exciting day when the new tenants at last moved into the new homes that they had waited for so long.

Over the years Wrexham has put a number of clearance plans into operation, such as the large housing developments in Acton, built during the 1930s, and the Queens Park estate, developed in the 1950s. Various private housing has long been available in Wrexham, and a number of private developments were constructed during the 1960s.

# Events & Occasions

THE WREXHAM FARMERS' CHARITY SALES WERE ESTABLISHED DURING WARTIME

A nice little crowd has turned out to bid at the Wrexham Farmers' Charity Sale, organised by the Union. The charity sales were established during wartime in support of organisations such as the Red Cross, and were well attended by people from the farming and butchers community. A number of gentlemen farmers were among the crowd; the young farmer on the left is very smart in his jodhpurs, jacket and trilby.

The auctioneers that day were likely to have been Jones & Son of Wrexham; the gentleman on the podium, hat in hand, and the man beside him holding a clipboard were probably representatives of the firm - was one of these gentlemen Mr Fred Jones himself? A wide selection of produce was to be sold at the Smithfield: poultry, both oven-dressed and alive, sheep and lambs, calves and pigs were all on offer along with cheese, butter, eggs and even garden plants. The little black and white dog wears a label - is he also for sale? And the young boy holding the notice looks as unhappy as if he, too, were going to be disposed of at auction! The Smithfield has now disappeared from Wrexham, and the Mecca Social Club today occupies the same site.

**Left:** The laying of the foundation stone is a historic moment in the life of any building, but this time, though we have the photographic record of this historic moment, we do not know what building was being constructed: well-informed readers will no doubt let us know. The date was the 11th October 1956, and doing the honours that day was George W Romney, who was president of the American Motors Corporation. Mr Romney was probably the gentleman in pin-stripe trousers (rare as hen's teeth today), watching as a few final adjustments were made to his handiwork. It is interesting to note that the flat cap worn by the builder in the background is the hardest hat in evidence in the photograph, and wellingtons are his preferred footwear. 'No hat, no boots, no job' is the slogan that reflects today's strict emphasis on workers' safety, but even as recently as the 1950s employees undertook many dangerous jobs every day without gauntlets, safety glasses, hard hats or protective clothing of any kind, and reflected very little on the risk factor. In fact, in some occupations it was regarded as being somewhat less than macho to wear protective clothing.

**Below:** Happy and excited, the crowd awaits the passing of the Queen's procession in July 1953, some of them claiming their seat many hours beforehand just to get a glimpse of Her Majesty - and hopefully a wave - as she was driven by in her Daimler. When the Queen was crowned in a Westminster Abbey service on 2nd June 1953, a mere eight years after the end of World War Two, the nation relaxed for the first time and really went to town on the celebrations that welcomed the Queen to the throne. Each town and city, every village institute and church, held their own event, which could range from a simple street party to a big parade. The pageantry of the coronation is well-remembered by a nation who viewed the coronation on television. The sight of the new queen being anointed with oil and having the crown placed upon her head is one which few can forget. Many are not aware that the Queen's coronation dress was itself symbolic, being embroidered with the emblems of the Dominions - India, Canada, New Zealand and Australia. When the ceremony was over, the Queen rode happily back to the palace in her golden coach, wearing the crown and carrying the orb and sceptre.

What a welcome the Queen received from these children when she stopped off at Wrexham on her Coronation Tour of Wales! These youngsters were among the thousands who cheered and shouted for Her Majesty, waving their Union Jacks as well as their Welsh national flags. Some of the children are wearing uniform, perhaps Brownies and Cubs. Others appear to be in school caps and uniforms. The bright and cheerful print skirts worn by some of these girls are typical of 1950s fashions, as are the hair ribbons, hair slides - and even gloves. Forty years ago, gloves were an essential part of a lady's wardrobe, and were a fashion accessory worn not just by mature women but by teenagers and even children. Back in 1953 a girl was not dressed up unless she was wearing a little hat, handbags, gloves, and perhaps a pair of shoes with Louis heels.

To many, the coronation of Queen Elizabeth II signalled the beginning of a 'new Elizabethan age', and the nation immediately took the young and pretty new queen to their hearts. The occasion even called for the writing of new songs; perhaps some readers will remember 'Let's all be new Elizabethans'?

# A TRIP THROUGH THE 1960s

### WHAT'S ON?
*Television comedy came into its own in the 1960s, and many of the shows that were favourites then went on to become classics. 'On the Buses', 'Steptoe and Son', 'Till Death Us Do Part' and 'The Army Game' kept audiences laughing, while the incredible talents of Morecambe and Wise, the wit of Des O'Connor - often the butt of the duo's jokes - and the antics of Benny Hill established them for ever in the nation's affections.*

### GETTING AROUND
*The 2nd March 1969 was a landmark in the history of aviation. The Anglo-French supersonic airliner Concorde took off for the first time from Toulouse in France. Concorde, which can cruise at almost twice the speed of sound, was designed to fly from London to New York in an incredible three hours twenty minutes. The event took place just weeks after the Boeing 747, which can carry 500 passengers to Concorde's modest 100, made its first flight.*

### THE WORLD AT LARGE
*'One giant leap for mankind' was taken on 20th July 1969, when Neil Armstrong made history as the first man to set foot on the moon. During the mission he and fellow-astronaut 'Buzz' Aldrin collected rock and soil samples, conducted scientific experiments - and had a lot of fun jumping around in the one-sixth gravity. Twenty-one hours and thirty-seven minutes after their landing they took off again in their lunar module 'Eagle' to rejoin Apollo II which was orbiting above them, proudly leaving the American flag on the Moon's surface.*

The Queen's visit to Wrexham was such a special occasion that many people took their own chairs to sit on (or perhaps to stand on if they happened to be at the back!). The good-natured crowd are here seen dispersing after the procession has gone by, threading their way past the soldiers who still remain at attention. It had been a long wait for these people; many of them had been so anxious to see the Queen in the flesh that they began to gather along the route of the procession an incredible seven hours before the royal party was expected to arrive in the town. The railway station itself was a riot of colour for the occasion, and the red carpet was unrolled across the platform for Her Majesty's arrival. Her train was met by Col J C Wynne-Finch MC JP, the Queen's Lieutenant for Denbighshire along with the Mayor and Deputy Mayor, before the party departed for Llwyn Isaf. The roads along the procession route had been closed to traffic almost an hour beforehand. The coronation gave everyone a chance to declare their loyalty to the Queen - and it was party time in Wrexham. Garlands and banners were hung in windows, lines of bunting stretched across every street, and though the weather on the big day was inclined to be cool and rather damp, it didn't stop the children from enjoying their street parties.

The 10th July 1953 was a never to be forgotten day in the history of Wrexham, when the Queen's grand Coronation Tour included the town on its itinerary. Thousands upon thousands of people turned out to welcome the Queen - crowned a mere five weeks previously - and her husband the Duke of Edinburgh to Wrexham. The Queen looks genuinely happy as to the strains of the National Anthem she is escorted by the Mayor, Councillor Herbert Jennings, to the specially constructed dais at Llwyn Isaf, itself a riot of colour for the occasion. Behind, with the immaculately-dressed Prince Philip, is the Deputy Mayor Councillor Eric McMahon - who looks rather as if he is about to do the Queen a mischief; it is to be hoped that Her Majesty did not stop suddenly!

Elegant as ever, the Queen was wearing an outfit in the light summery colours that suited her so well; her dress was lilac brocaded taffeta figured in blue, while her stylish loose coat was lilac pink with a lining that matched the dress. Her half-hat was made of pale pink flowers, and a pair of long black gloves, black handbag and black peep-toe shoes completed the outfit.

The large number of invited guests who were privileged to attend the event were nevertheless given rules to comply with. They were asked to be seated in their places at Llwyn Isaf by three o'clock - and they were strictly forbidden to take photographs of the royal couple. After prominent citizens were presented to Her Majesty the royal couple signed the visitor's book. Local schoolgirl Megan Lewis's friends were no doubt green with envy when she presented a beautiful bouquet of flowers to the Queen before she left for Llangollen with the rest of the royal party at 3.50, where they attended the Eisteddfodd.

**Left:** The Queen and the Duke of Edinburgh included the War Memorial Hospital in Rhosddu Road in their Coronation Tour of Wales, and to the patients, staff and crowds of spectators 10th July 1953 was a very special day. The hospital was decked in red, white and blue for the occasion, with flags and bunting fluttering everywhere and banners with 'E II R' proclaiming their loyalty to the newly-crowned Queen. Rows of nurses were ranked above a number of beds that had been moved out on to the pavement to give the patients a ringside view; we see that the Queen's Daimler has just drawn level with them. A police car leads the procession of official cars.

Thousands of children lined the streets with their parents to welcome Her Majesty to Wrexham that day; 5,000 of them gathered at Llwyn Isaf alone. Their greeting was so enthusiastic that the Queen was impressed, actually commenting on it afterwards.

Unlike her father King George VI, the young and pretty new Queen had begun her training for the throne early, when Edward VIII's abdication in 1936 made her the heir presumptive to the throne. She was only 14 years old when she broadcast messages of encouragement to the children of war-torn Britain, and as the war progressed she gradually took on more and more public duties.

**Above:** Princess Alexandra touched everyone's hearts during her visit to Wrexham on 26th May 1961, when she opened the new Guild Hall. The Princess simply refused to be hurried along, and to the delight of the thousands who turned out to see her, she spent time chatting to people in the crowd. She made an unscheduled stop at the War Memorial Hospital, where the entire children's ward had been moved out to the pavement. Their beds and thirteen cots lined the roadside, and to the children's delight Princess Alexandra stopped to say hello to most of them. In the town space on the pavements was at a premium and many of those relegated to the back rows resorted to bringing out step ladders and stools so that they could get a better view! Stores with upper windows facing the route gave many of their vantage points to senior citizens, whose only disappointment was with the Princess's closed car; they had hoped she would be in an open-topped vehicle.

The 4th Battalion of the Royal Welch Fusiliers TA formed the Princess's Guard of Honour, and Corporal Gordon Gregory was on parade with the regiment's mascot, a goat unimaginatively named Billy. After ceremonially opening the Guild Hall door with a gold key the Princess signed the visitors book - and departed for the Memorial Hall for tea.

## THE ROYAL WELCH FUSILIERS HAVE BEEN CLOSELY LINKED WITH WREXHAM SINCE 1877

Everyone loves a parade, especially if there is a band to keep everyone in step with a rousing march, and back in 1954 a crowd had gathered at the junction of King Street and Grove Park Lane to watch the band of the Royal Welch Fusiliers march past in the direction of the nearby hospital. The smartly turned-out young ladies and boys on the right were perhaps cadets with the AFC, or were perhaps part of the Observer Corps. It is not clear what event is being celebrated, but a little bunting is in evidence in the background, and some of the children are waving the Union Jack.

This view has changed vastly in recent years; today the recently built Yale College stands on the left, though the house in the background is still standing. Further along is the Dewi Sant chapel in RhosDdu Road, while further back still the trees would one day be replaced by Wrexham's excellent new library.

The Royal Welch Fusiliers have been closely linked with Wrexham since 1877. In the early days the men were housed in temporary billets, but when Florence Nightingale returned from the Crimea and raised a public outcry against the insanitary living conditions of British soldiers, the regiment's first permanent barracks was built in Wrexham.

# Wartime

In 1939 Prime Minister Neville Chamberlain had made his announcement to the waiting people of Britain that '...this country is at war with Germany.' This war would be different from other wars. This time planes had the ability to fly further and carry a heavier load, and air raids were fully expected. Air raid shelters were obviously going to be needed, and shelters were built on open places across the town.

By the time war was declared an army of volunteers of both sexes had already been recruited to form an Air Raid Protection service. At first ARP personnel were unpaid volunteers but when war broke out in September 1939 they became paid staff. It was their job to

patrol specified areas, making sure that no chinks of light broke the blackout restrictions, checking the safety of local residents, being alert for gas attacks, air raids and unexploded bombs. The exceptional work done by Air Raid Wardens in dealing with incendiaries, giving first aid to the injured, helping to rescue victims from their bombed-out properties, clearing away rubble, and a thousand and one other tasks became legendary; during the second world war nearly as many private citizens were killed as troops - and many of them were the gallant ARP wardens.

In July the Local Defence Volunteers were renamed the Home Guard, and by the following year were a force to be reckoned with. Television programmes such as 'Dad's Army' have unfortunately associated the Home Guard with comedy, but in fact they performed much important work. The Guard posted sentries to watch for possible aircraft or parachute landings at likely spots such as disused aerodromes, golf courses on the outskirts of towns, local parks

and racecourses. They manned anti-aircraft rocket guns, liaised with other units and with regular troops, set up communications and organised balloon barrages.

Other preparations were hastily made around the towns and cities of Britain. Place names and other identifying marks were obliterated to confuse the enemy about exactly where they were. Notices went up everywhere giving good advice to citizens on a number of issues. 'Keep Mum - she's not so dumb' warned people to take care what kind of information they passed on, as the person they were speaking to could be an enemy.

Older readers will remember how difficult it was to find certain items in the shops during the war; combs, soap, cosmetics, hairgrips, elastic, buttons, zips - all were virtually impossible to buy as factories that once produced these items had been turned over to war work. Stockings were in short supply, and resourceful women resorted to colouring their legs with gravy browning or with a mixture of sand and water. Beetroot juice was found to be a good substitute for lipstick.

Clothes rationing was introduced in 1941, and everyone had 66 coupons per year. Eleven coupons would buy a dress, and sixteen were needed for a coat. The number of coupons was later reduced to 40 per person. People were required to save material where they could - ladies' hemlines went up considerably, and skirts were not allowed to have lots of pleats. Some found clever ways around the regulations by using materials that were not rationed. Blackout material could be embroidered and made into blouses or skirts, and dyed sugar sacks were turned into curtains.

**Above:** War had been declared, and every citizen of Britain, young and old, male and female, was called upon to put his or her back into the war effort. Those who did not go into military service of one kind or another worked in factories, dug for victory, gave up their aluminium baths and saucepans, joined organisations and aided in any way they could. These boys were not going to be left out; they might be too young to fight but while there were sandbags to be filled they were going to do their bit to protect their school building. Thousands of sandbags were used during World War II to protect the country and its beautiful civic buildings.

**Left:** A proud father poses for the camera with his latest arrival. The baby had not arrived from Mars, in fact the 'arrival' was not a baby at all, but an anti-gas attack suit which was compulsory for babies in the United Kingdom during the Second World War. An air pump at the side of the suit enabled anxious parents to replenish the supply of air to the precious package inside. It is said that most babies were less than enthusiastic abut the prospect of being encased in the suit - and who could blame them? The picture was taken in 1939. In the event there was never any gas attack on British soil during the course of the second world war.

Before World War II many of these men had never before wielded so much as a broom handle in anger, but even so they were all prepared to defend Britain in the event of invasion. These marchers were the men of the Wrexham Home Guard, and the salute is being taken on the steps of the Technical College. The unobscured traffic sign in the background indicates that this was after the war had ended, so this occasion could have been the disbanding of the Home Guard. When war broke out Sir Anthony Eden, who was the Secretary of State for War, appealed in a radio broadcast for men between 17 and 65 to make up a new force of amateur soldiers, ordinary people who were outside military age or who were prevented from joining the forces because they were in reserve occupations. Within an hour or two the first men were putting their names down. At first the new defence force had to improvise; there were no weapons to spare and men had to rely on sticks, shotguns handed in by local people, and on sheer determination . Despite the fact that weapons and uniforms did not become available for several months, the LDV trained hard to meet the standards required of them.

The force, even if amateur, was very well organised. If parachutes were seen landing, the local church bells would be rung to summon the unpaid volunteers from their normal jobs of work. Guidelines were laid down as to what type of parachutists should and should not be shot at; fewer than six parachutists could well be our own aircraft personnel baling out of a damaged aircraft, so the Home Guard were instructed not to shoot them until they were certain who they were shooting at!

**Left:** The food preparation area of Operation Jupiter, and Mrs Hughes and Mrs Slater, wearing spotless white aprons, are already busy with the wooden spoon and enormous bowl. Major H Brougham and Major Ivor Watkins are the two army observers who have paused to have a chat with the ladies. A much-respected agency, the WVS did much sterling work during World War II, running mobile canteens, caring for evacuees and refugees, distributing clothes to those in need and performing a thousand and one vital jobs. Her Majesty the Queen paid tribute to the work of the WVS in 1966 by adding 'Royal' to the title. The agency continue to play a vital role in providing care where needed; during 1998 they provided 12 million meals on wheels to 100,000 recipients and assisted at 128 real-life emergencies. After the death of Diana, Princess of Wales, the WRVS provided refreshments for people who queued for up to 12 hours to sign the books of condolence. And it was WRVS members who helped to clear up the incredible 25,000 tonnes of flowers after the event.

**Below:** A WVS camp back in September 1957 - and not a plastic sheet in sight! Exercise Jupiter - obviously staged near a disused railway line - was well underway for these Wrexham volunteers. Mass food preparation was largely what the exercise was about, and the rather friendly sign on the side of the lorry in the background tells us informally that this was a 'food fixing squad'. The women were practising their field skills in order to cope with large-scale emergencies. They had to learn to utilise any materials that were to hand; one of the tables is constructed from three planks of wood supported by four drums. Note the field oven on the left, which is a 40-gallon drum with a stove-pipe chimney, supported on a brick base. Steam drifts from the chimneys of half a dozen boilers; what was on the menu that day? The equipment may have been rough and ready, but hygiene was certainly not neglected; readers with a sharp eye might pick out a 'Wash your Hands' notice on the front of the canvas awning. It is interesting to note the mobile and easily-erected sectional corrugated building in the background (toilets, perhaps?); in a similar situation today, a portakabin would be used.

Slaving over a hot stove was an occupation these members of the Wrexham Women's Voluntary Service practised in their spare time as well as at home! This was Exercise Jupiter, held on 29th September 1957, and the army observers attending the exercise would appear to be about ready for a nice cup of tea from one of the large urns.

The WVS was founded to help people in need, and part of their work has always been attending emergencies in peace as well as in wartime. At any time the service has to be ready to cope with full-scale disaster situations, and this involves preparing thousands of cups of tea and huge quantities of food. All this cannot be done, of course, without prior planning and organisation so regular exercises help the members to establish a well-organised system of working. Exercises are still held regularly today, though the venue is more likely to be a school hall or a community centre than a camp under canvas. The old field kitchen equipment has now been packed away - though is still kept on hand - just in case!

The WRVS still perform vital emergency help. In December 1997 800 homes were evacuated in Cadoxton, South Wales, after a rail tanker carrying toxic chemicals was derailed. In conjunction with other agencies, the WRVS set up rest centres at two leisure centres in Barry to cope with the 160 evacuees (and 18 pets!).

Wide and genuine smiles were on the faces of these ladies - even the dog appears to grin for the photographer! They were all members of the Women's Royal Army Corps T A, 322 (North Wales). The year was 1957, and all of them, except perhaps for their commanding officer would be reservists working in shops, schools, factories or as housewives. For a variety of reasons they would join their local branch of the WRAC. Some had strong family connections in the regular or the territorial army, while others simply wanted to do their bit for the country. Whatever their reason, the ladies usually found

great fulfilment in their life as part time soldiers. Traditionally they provided female backup for the armed forces, releasing men from support services working as telephonists, typists, radio operators, operations clerks and cooks. For one night a week they would learn and practise new skills at their local depot, putting their new skills to use at weekend camps. Life in the WRAC offered them a chance to do something totally different from their civilian life; there they had the opportunity for training and education, for excitement and adventure - and perhaps even the chance to travel.

# Shopping spree

Opened in 1871 in Hope Street, the successful Dutton's Sig Ar Ro grocery stores eventually extended their premises to No 2 High Street. The Candy Corner kiosk captured passing trade in sweets and cigarettes, while the rest of the premises were devoted to groceries and provisions. In the mid 1970s the building was demolished to make way for a building society. Small grocery chains such as Duttons and the Maypole, who established themselves in Hope Street in the early years of the 20th century, were the traditional way to shop, and customers would queue to be served while the assistant weighed out butter from a huge slab and sliced bacon while you waited - a far cry from today's plastic packs! In those early days goods such as biscuits, sugar and dried fruit were all weighed out for the individual customer. People might have to wait a while longer to be served, but at least they had the benefit of personal attention from the staff. Things were to remain that way until the mid-1950s, when self-service shopping began to catch on. The trend started slowly, but it was the thin end of the wedge. Over the last forty or so years there has been a shift towards supermarkets and out-of-town shopping.

**Above:** As early as 1940 - the date given for this photograph - it was necessary to have a one-way system for Wrexham's traffic, and the 'No Entry' signs in Hope Street carry the famous AA logo. The way these shoppers overflow from the pavement into the roadway, however, emphasises the fact that heavy traffic in 1940 bore no resemblance to 1990s-style heavy traffic! Many readers will remember Sig Ar Ro on the corner of Hope Street and High Street. Duttons Sig Ar Ro was a landmark in the town for many years; the Chester firm Duttons

OLD STYLE GROCERY SHOPS MAY HAVE MEANT YOU WAITED LONGER - BUT AT LEAST THE SERVICE WAS GOOD

opened their Wrexham branch as far back as 1871. Remember Candy Corner, the sweets and cigarette kiosk that once occupied this corner of Duttons? In the distance is Burton the tailors at the junction of Queen Street with Hope Street, and the town's second branch of the well-known gents' outfitters can be seen on the left in Hope Street. The sharp-eyed will have spotted the Union Jack hanging outside Woolworths on the right. We can not be sure what the occasion was, but as World War II was just getting into its stride, perhaps the flag was placed there simply as a patriotic gesture?

**Above:** *This row of shops almost opposite the museum can still be seen today, though little else in Regent Street remains as it was back in the 1930s when this photograph was taken. The businesses have changed, of course; here the Britannic Assurance Company occupied the first shop, and the gable end is utilised to advertise Clarks wedding cars and taxis. The business in the centre is Thorntons stationery office, and perhaps - though this is by no means certain - the shop at the far end was a tobacconist. The building on the corner of King Street is the old Imperial Hotel; the Job Centre was to eventually replace it. When this photograph was taken the Majestic Cinema, just off-picture to the right, was still packing in the punters. In recent years the popular wine bar trend converted the old cinema into the Elihu Yale Wine Bar. Unlike many similar establishments elsewhere that were given such trendy names as The Blue Parrot or The Grinning Rat, at least The Elihu Yale commemorates the name of one of Wrexham's well-known local characters. Yale's generosity led to the founding of Yale University in Connecticut, whose chapel tower is a replica of the pinnacled tower of St Giles' church.*

**Right:** *A busy day in High Street was captured for posterity back in 1945. Victory in Europe had just been - or was about to be - declared, and there was a new sense of hope in the air in Wrexham. The two bobbies on the beat in the foreground of the photograph appear to have little to worry about; compared with today the 1940s was a comparatively law-abiding decade.*

*Crime figures were far lower back then, and in a twelve-month period the Wrexham force might have around four instances of 'taking away vehicles without the owner's consent'. A few Saturday night incidents in the town centre might have been as much excitement as they could expect; Wrexham has always had its fair share of local breweries and public houses! 'Bents Ales and Stouts', advertised on the right of the photograph, was one such local brewery.*

*An interesting feature of the photograph is the number of white-helmeted motor bike riders in High Street.*

*Motor cyclists were not at that time required by law to wear helmets (and rarely did), so these riders were likely to have belonged to the Royal Welch Fusiliers, on their way back to their barracks in Kings Mills Road.*

Divided by railings and a wide roadway, rivals face each other across High Street, though one hopes that it was not with pistols drawn! The popular Burtons gents outfitters had two branches in the town; the other one was in Hope Street. The Fifty Shilling Tailors was established during the 1920s, supplying affordable suits, primarily for servicemen . The sum of 50/- (two pounds ten shillings in today's currency, if not in value!) would have paid for a smart and very serviceable suit of clothes, a must for any man being interviewed for a job, particularly as a salesman or a clerk. Some

time in the 1950s the full name Fifty Shilling Tailors was abbreviated to 'FST', and the firm was later taken over by Colliers. A number of readers will no doubt remember their jolly little TV jingle informing viewers that John Colliers was 'the window to watch'! Gentlemen's outfitting has long been a trade to attract many rivals: Alkit (who specialised in cheaper clothing), Greenwoods, Hepworths, Hornes, Moss Bros, Austin Reed, and at the top end of the market, Hector Powe. The rival firm Hepworths eventually managed to acquire the services of the Queen's own designer.

Hope Street was empty of traffic though busy with shoppers in this photograph which dates from 1950. Boots the chemist, on the far left of the picture, had a row of rather nice lamps which are in themselves worth a mention. Next door is the Westminster Building which was distinguished by having been built by William Low, the very first pioneer of the Channel Tunnel. Though test bores were dug as far back as 1959, the rail link between England and France was not opened until 6th May 1994. Few people appear to be taking notice of the rather unusual sign near

Williams & Morgan's tailors that advises them to walk on the left of the footpath; above it an arrow directs travellers to turn right to reach the LNER station and car park. Hope Street has always had its fair share of pubs; within a hundred yards or so we have the Black Lion, the Old Kings Head and on the far right on the corner of Priory Street, the Horse and Jockey. A popular watering-hole in the town, the Horse and Jockey's roof was thatched at the time of this photograph, giving it an olde-worlde appearance. The Abbey National eventually took its place.

*This view of Regent Street in 1963 is one that will bring back many memories. Do you remember, for example, Stevens' Cafe - and the furore that followed its sudden and inadvised demolition? Almost literally overnight the cafe disappeared from the street - and the firm was later fined for its hasty action! Their own van stands outside in this photograph, and the advert advises passers-by to 'Meet your friends at Stevens' Cafe - coffee, lunch or tea'. Readers will perhaps also remember buying shoes from Olivers on the left, or a special gift of a watch or jewellery from Walton's next door. The kettle hanging outside*

*Walter Roberts shop might lead some to suppose that this was a teashop; established in the early years of the 20th century, Walter Roberts was in fact Wrexham's leading ironmonger, a large establishment where you could buy anything from a clock to a saucepan and from a lamp to a picture frame. A banner draped across the front of the facing buildings advertises the fact that the celebrated Halle Orchestra, under the conductor Sir John Barbirolli, would be playing at William Aston Hall at 7pm on Saturday 23rd May. Today the hall is still privileged to be host to the Halle.*

# At work

**Left:** The staff of North Wales Power (which with nationalisation in 1948 became the Merseyside and North Wales Electricity Board) at Willow Works are the subject of this photograph, which unfortunately is undated. A number of the men are still very much alive and part of the community: Dick Parry is the man just off-centre wearing a trilby hat - the only one wearing glasses; above him on the far right of the back row is Bobby Hewitt. Note the Electrical Union 'Light and Liberty' badges that many of these men are proudly displaying on their jackets; Dick Parry was the Trade Union official. Note, too, the bib and brace overalls, popular workwear during the 1940s and 50s, being worn by a number among the work force. The young man first on the left on the back row is wearing army battledress, which could indicate that the war had not long been over when they posed for the camera.

Situated next to the River Gwenfro, Willow Works was in Tuttle Street, next to the old baths. Today of course the site lies on the ring road, and the whole area has been beautifully landscaped as the river walk.

**Below:** The immature trees in this view of the Guild Hall, along with the fine old cars in the car park, would indicate that the photograph was taken in the early 1960s. Note the lack of an identifying sign; it seems strange that a building so important to Wrexham should lack even a coat of arms!

The designs of the cars pictured here present an interesting contrast between the somewhat austere lines of the Ford Popular, typical of earlier decades, and the lighter, sleeker lines that developed in the post-war years, when colour was introduced into motor car design. The sleek Ford Consul, the Wolseley 1500, and the Hillman Minx are desired as classic cars today, while in its day the Ford Popular was a very affordable little vehicle. More than one among our readers will no doubt remember the 'Ford Pop' with fondness as their very first car. Do you remember the strange layout of the gears, with reverse where first gear would be on other cars? And the hand-brake placed below the dashboard? And the vacuum wipers that gave up when you put your foot down and flogged away like mad when you eased off the accelerator? All part of this great little vehicle's character.

## PREFABS PRESENTED A QUICKLY-BUILT SOLUTION TO THE HOUSING SHORTAGE OF THE 40s AND 50s

This hawk's eye view of the Denbighshire Technical College during construction reveals a landscape that has vastly changed in recent years. Mold Road cuts across the lower half of the photograph, with Maes Gwyn housing estate in the foreground. Robins supporters will immediately spot what's missing at the Wrexham Football Club - there's not a floodlight in sight! A dozen or so Crosville buses can be seen parked behind the bus depot, while Maes Gwyn Masonic Hall, renowned for its banqueting and conference facilities, is 'next door' along. On the right edge of the photograph is the start of the estate of prefabs that provided families with single-storey housing until recent years. Prefabs presented a quickly-built though temporary solution to the country-wide housing shortage of the 40s and 50s. People from older properties were used to doing without bathrooms and using outside toilets, and the surprisingly spacious little bungalows with bathrooms, separate toilets, built-in cupboards and drawers and modern kitchens quickly became popular. Prefabs were originally built to last around ten years but in many towns they were still occupied well into the 1960s and beyond. They were gradually phased out and replaced by new housing estates.

# Where the tissue of success is made

Wrexham Industrial Estate was built in 1939 to house a Royal Ordnance munitions factory. After the war, the premises became available for industrial use; the spacious and easily accessible site made the accommodation suitable for a large company, and Johnson and Johnson, a major manufacturer of Band-aid, bandages and other household medical and sanitary supplies, moved to the Wrexham Industrial Estate in 1946.

Johnson and Johnson continued to operate from here for over a decade, until in the late 50s the company was taken over by Smith and Nephew, who manufactured similar goods and traded as the Velvet Crepe Paper Co. At about this time that the tissue market in the UK was just beginning to take off. Looking back, it is rather surprising that although paper had been made by machine since the beginning of the 19th century and had quickly been exploited in various forms as a writing and printing material, and as a packaging material in such forms as cardboard boxes, brown paper and greaseproof paper, soft tissue was a relatively late development. Once introduced, however, disposable paper towels and paper handkerchiefs quickly became popular as their advantages as hygienic and convenient alternatives to their fabric counterparts were recognised; and soft toilet tissue, too, was soon preferred by many households as it was gentler to use than the

harder 'Bronco' type tissue which the previous generation had favoured. The market's ready acceptance of these products was a clear indication that the new tissue industry could look forward to considerable expansion. In 1962, following negotiations between Smith and Nephew, Wiggins Teape, Peter Dixons and Inveresk, a Group was formed, which after further discussion settled on the name of British Tissues. One of British Tissues' first actions was to purchase a number of small machines for making tissues.

Tissues are made by 'converting' paper; this means cutting, folding or rolling, and packing, so that the tissues emerge from the factory already packaged and ready to be marketed. The machines which carry out these functions are known as Paper Converting Machines, or PCMs, and these machines vary in the width of rolls they can produce and the speed at which they run. In the early days of tissue manufacture, there was little automation in the factory; many of the processes were carried out manually, and before the advent of fork-lift trucks, warehousing and loading involved a great deal of manual handling of heavy boxes. As technology developed, more automation was introduced into the various factory processes, and larger and faster paper converting machines became available. In the 1970s the company made the decision to purchase two fastline PCMs; these were, at the time, the first two machines of their type in Europe. In the 1980s, as industrial technology continued to advance, lines were improved to incorporate computerised quality controls. Then, through a merger in 1993, British Tissues acquired a tabletop manufacture plant in Tottenham; tabletop manufacture is the term used for items such as tablecloths, napkins, plates, cups, cutlery and children's party products. The Tottenham plant had suffered from lack of investment over a period of time, and had been allowed to become antiquated and therefore expensive to run. British Tissues transferred the operation to Wrexham, where it was able to

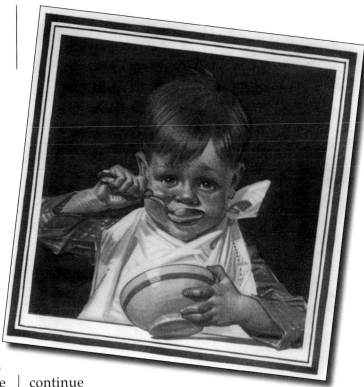

continue tabletop manufacture more efficiently. These products are marketed by the group under the tradename Deeko.

In 1997, following a take-over by James River, an international manufacturer of disposable paper products marketed by the Jamont group, the Wrexham factory became Fort James and was brought to the forefront of the industry. A new facial tissue bretting line was installed to increase production. Further major investment was made in 1996, with the installation of new machinery to change one of the fast lines into high speed interleaf facial tissue production, so that in 1998 Wrexham became the sole UK site for producing facial tissues for the UK and European markets. All major supermarkets' own-branded tissues are made here, including Safeway, Kwiksave, Gateway, Boots, Tesco, Sainsburys etc, as is Dixcel, Fort James' own brand. In total, 30 per cent of the UK and European market is supplied from here; this represents 2.5 million cases of tissue, with 24 boxes in a case, and involves the conversion of approximately 14,000 tons of paper.

The paper which is converted at Wrexham comes from the company's own plants in Bridgend and in France. As a major paper manufacturer, Fort James places great importance on safeguarding the environment, and has a world-wide programme of educating communities on forestry and environmental issues.

*Above: An early advertising promotion.* **Left:** *A Johnson & Johnson conference meeting in the 1950s.*

Paper is made from wood pulp, recycled waste paper and water; other fibres and additives are sometimes included to produce special kinds of paper, for example to make whiter, smoother paper, or to make paper with extra strength, elasticity or softness. The waste paper which is to be used must be sorted to remove any string, wire, plastic or other extraneous material and impurities. Originally, the problems of sorting the waste paper meant that it could be used only in the production of lower quality paper, but the improved techniques in separation and purification which Fort James employs mean that the company can also use recovered paper in the manufacture of premium quality products. Worldwide, Fort James uses nearly 2.4 million tons of recycled paper each year, and invests heavily in energy conservation measures. Water is recycled through secondary waste water treatment facilities, resulting in very pure discharge water. The company is deeply committed to its environmental policy, and marks a clear distinction between its own on-going efforts and investment to ensure that its products are designed and produced in

an environmentally sound manner, and superficial "green" marketing claims which it dismisses as environmental opportunism.

Worldwide, Fort James' range of paper products is extensive. The company has approximately 29,000 employees and more than 65 manufacturing facilities in North America, Western Europe, Russia and China. As well as tissues and tabletop goods, Fort James produces innovative folding cartons for the packaging of many different kinds of goods, all of which have their own particular requirements; for instance, pharmaceutical items such as tablets need special packaging, and the pre-packed food industry has special requirements including special containers for microwaveable foods which promote browning. The company also manufactures communications papers such as printing, publishing and office copy paper. Its products are bought both by the household consumer and by the business and industrial sector, and appear under many familiar brandnames; besides Deeko and Dixcel, they include Lotus, KittenSoft, Nouvelle, Soft 'n' Gentle, Eureka! and Word Pro.

Whilst Fort James at Wrexham is able to enjoy the benefits of being part of a large multinational enterprise, decisions relating to the running of the factory and the implementation of changes are made at a local level, which means that it can continue to build on the traditional strengths which come from having been established on its present site for a long time. It is this combination of the knowledge and experience of the factory's staff with the investment power of the parent company and the support of the European Research and Technology Centre in France which has ensured the continuing success and growth of the Wrexham factory. The paper tissue industry has been subject to continual technological development, and a comprehensive programme of investment has been necessary to ensure that the plant can continue to improve the quality of its products and the efficiency of the manufacturing process, without causing a negative impact on the environment. Thanks to the success of Fort James, Wrexham, customers worldwide can enjoy the quality and value of the new softer paper which is now being manufactured, safe in the knowledge that they are buying an environmentally-friendly product from a company which is committed to responsible stewardship of the environment, protection of employee health, and assurance of product safety.

*Above: Some of the company's products.*
*Left: The site today.*
*Facing page, top: A children's Christmas party from the 1950s.*
*Facing page, bottom: A view of the No. 1 Factory dating from the 1950s.*

# Acrefair: where success is in the air

In 1996 Air Products Limited drew up plans to extend its facilities within the existing Acrefair works. This attracted great interest, not only from the business community, but from local archaeologists and historians, because it was known that the remains of an ironworks complex dating back to the 18th century was located within their site. During the works, various features of significance were discovered, including an old, capped coal shaft, old kilns and some structural remains of the former ironworks. The history of this site has been extensively researched by Air Products Limited, who took the premises over in 1957, and makes fascinating reading.

The site at Acrefair, part of Cefn Mawr, was first put to industrial use almost two centuries ago by Edward Lloyd Rowland. The early 19th century was something of a boom time for local iron manufacture, following the opening of the Ellesmere Canal. Lloyd Rowland built two 43' high blast furnaces and a large double casting house, subsequently adding a rolling mill, 16 or so puddling furnaces and a warehouse. He also sank nearly 30 coal pits, mostly in the Ruabon areas some two miles from Acrefair; indeed, he seemed to have all the ingredients necessary for a large-scale, successful

ironworks, but unfortunately, perhaps as a result of fluctuating prices of pig iron during the Napoleonic Wars, Lloyd Rowland went bankrupt in 1823. In 1825 the furnaces and the pits were purchased by the British Iron Company, and a very stormy period in the history of this site began.

The British Iron Company owned a large ironworks in Abersychan, Monmouthshire, and had sufficient funds to invest some £140,000 in the Ruabon works during its first years of ownership. The 1830s and 40s were a difficult time for industry, and many businesses failed; in 1841 Mr Wood, who worked for the British Iron Company, reported that out of the 20 blast furnaces in north-east Wales only six, including one of the two at Acrefair, were still in production.

At the time, the company was considered to be a harsh employer. Payment at Ruabon was by the 'truck system'. This system was used by other mineowners as well, but it was said that the British Iron Company's system was the worst. Under the 'truck system', a

*Below: Early 1960's view of the machine shop - now converted to the Apprentice Training School.*

was by trying to sell food outside the mining community for cash. The women at Ruabon also complained that they had to queue for hours to be served at the tommy shops, which reduced the hours they were able to work.

So by November 1930, when the Friendly Associated Coalminers' Union formed its first Welsh Lodge at Bagilt Backel on the North Wales Coast, the miners at Ruabon had a grievance. The first action of the new Union Lodge took place at Hawarden, a village about 15 miles north of Ruabon, where the miners went on strike in support of their demand for a minimum wage of 3s 0d per week for skilled workers and 2s 6d for the lowest grade workers.

Their demand was met in full, putting the Union representatives in a strong position when they toured the neighbouring collieries to recruit members. A rumour spread that a general strike was planned for 27 December, 1930, and the Denbighshire County Yeomanry, a volunteer peacekeeping force, was called in by Sir Watkin Williams Wynn, Lord Lieutenant of the County, and was sent to Rhos to disperse a large group of miners who had assembled to take the Union Oath. Two of the Union leaders were arrested but their colleagues rushed to free them and the crowd then reassembled on a nearby slag heap.

proportion of the miners' wages was paid in tickets or token money which could only be exchanged in the company's own shops, known as 'tommy shops'. This system was open to abuse by the mineowner. Taken to extremes, it could result in a miner's entire wage consisting of token money; the shops tended to charge extortionate prices - in 1831 the proprietors of the British Iron Company's tommy shop at Acrefair were prosecuted for selling sugar at 8d a pound instead of 5d, flannel at 1s 4d instead of 1s 0d, and for selling short weight - and the only way that wives could obtain necessities not available at the tommy shops

*Above:* *Vertical boring in the 'main' machine shop, 1960's.*
*Below:* *1965 photograph of storage area. The building on the right is the main machine shop, with the offices in the distance.*

There they were read the 'Riot Act' which provoked the boys and women to throw cinders at the troops. Warning shots were fired into the crowd, and a third arrest was made. The situation was defused by Sir Watkin who publicly reprimanded the troopers and ordered the release of the prisoners. The excitement over, the miners drifted home, but the Battle of Cinder Hill was not forgotten.

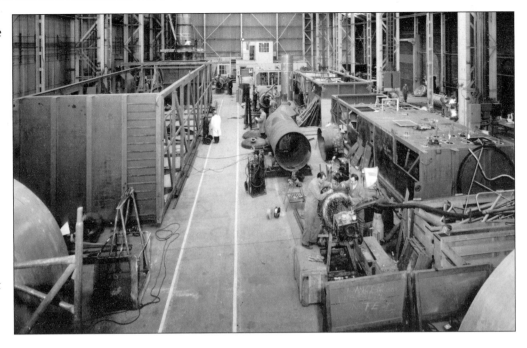

The following day the miners reassembled at Acrefair, in driving snow, to demonstrate against the British Iron Company's tommy shop. Again the Yeomanry was called in; again the Riot Act was read; and again Sir Watkin pacified the crowd by promising to arrange a meeting between the masters and a Union deputation. The meeting took place as promised at the Wynstay Arms Hotel, Ruabon, but the masters refused to make any concessions. It is said that the Manager, Mr Wood, sneered at the miners through the window as the meeting was going on. The miners were so incensed when they learned the outcome that they rushed the building;

Mr Wood was almost killed, and the story goes that he escaped from the hotel by disguising himself as a woman. Sir Watkin, who had not been present at the meeting, arranged for the employers to reconvene at his own house where he succeeded in persuading most of the employers to sign a document agreeing to the miners' demands. However, he was criticised by the Prime Minister, Lord Melbourne, for not taking action against the ring-leaders, and three Bow Street Runners were sent from Chester with an Infantry detachment to make an arrest.

Three men were apprehended and charged with assaulting Mr Wood, and although at their trial the British Iron Company pressed for their deportation, they were each sentenced to a year's imprisonment.

Having achieved victory at Ruabon, the Union turned its attention to neighbouring pits. The next few years saw numerous strikes and continual conflict between miners and masters, which eroded away support. Another factor in the Union's decline was that the Calvanistic Methodist Assembly in October 1831 forebade its members to join Trade Unions. The Union died out, and it was 50 years before a Union again began to play an important role in the Welsh pits.

In 1844 the North Wales Mineral Railway was opened, providing vital transport links and giving the industry a new lease of life. The British Iron Company became the new British Iron Company and the Acrefair

*Above:* 'Cold Boxes' being fabricated in Shop 3. The old pressure testing bay can just be seen at the far end of the shop.
*Left:* An aerial view of the modern site.

from this factory is in use in steel works in the UK, Korea, South Africa and Belgium. Other users include the semi conductor, petroleum and chemical industries.

The factory here at Ruabon manufactures a range of products from the largest distillation columns for cryogenic air separation, weighing up to 250 tonnes, to small storage tanks for liquid products. The columns are the core of the process which takes atmospheric air, compresses and dries it and cools it to minus 165°C where it is separated into its component parts, oxygen, nitrogen and argon. The gaseous products can be supplied to customer by pipeline directly into their factories from local air separation plants. These products can also be further compressed and supplied in cylinders for use in smaller quantities.

The oxygen, nitrogen and argon can also be liquified and then transported and stored in vacuum insulated storage tankers or tanks - which are also manufactured here.

On this site 270 people are employed either as craftspersons or supporting the activities associated with building these products.

Over the years there have been a number of extensions and modifications to allow the factory to expand for the different business needs and add to the production capabilities.

*Above & below: Air Separation units leaving Acrefair bound for the People's Republic of China.*

works increased production to 15,600 tons of iron a year by 1854. There were some problems with the quality of the iron, however; a new blast furnace was constructed in 1870 but was a failure. On November 22, 1970 there was an explosion which killed at least seven men and injured many more. After this only the puddling furnaces continued to be used, and the company closed down in 1888.

The site was then purchased in 1891 by Mr Hughes and Mr Lancaster, who moved their sewage handling business there from Chester. Many changes were made to the premises, including the installation of electric lighting; the business prospered and extended its activities into textile, mining and air compression machinery. In 1947 it was sold by Mr Wilfred Lancaster, who was by then sole owner, to the Butterley Company of Derby. In 1951 the Butterley Company negotiated an agreement with Air Products Incorporated of Allentown, Pennsylvania to manufacture oxygen plants under licence which led to a merger of the two companies in 1957. In October 1961 the Butterley Company withdrew from the partnership, leaving the company wholly owned by Air Products Incorporated.

Over the 42 years since its start in the UK the company has expanded both here, in Europe and in the Far East, supplying many different industries worldwide. Equipment

# Stylish tiles and the pavers favoured by the people of Wrexham

During the second half of the last century, coal was the most important industry in North Wales, with the North Wales coal seam which ran from the Point of Ayr to Ifton, near Oswestry, providing jobs for up to 45,000 workers; the Hafod Colliery alone, at its peak, employed some 2,000 miners. Mining operations also produced, as a by-product, clay, and around Ruabon the famous Ruabon Marl was found in quantity, so there sprang up in the area a number of companies making clay products. One of the first established and most well-known was J C Edwards, which started in 1850 and went on to become Britain's largest producer of terracotta, with factories at Pentybont and Acrefair.

In 1878 the Ruabon Coal Company, which owned Hafod Colliery, went into liquidation. The colliery was taken over by the Ruabon Coal and Coke Company, a new company formed by a Cornish-born businessman, Henry Dennis, who had first come to North Wales in 1850 to construct a tramway from the Llangollen Slate Quarries to the Shropshire Union Canal. He had then spent a short time in the lead mines in Spain before returning to North Wales to manage the Bryn y Rowan colliery. In 1857 he and his brother-in-law Walter Glennie had set up in partnership as Surveyors and Mining Engineers; when Walter Glennie left the partnership three years later Henry Dennis had continued on his own for a while before

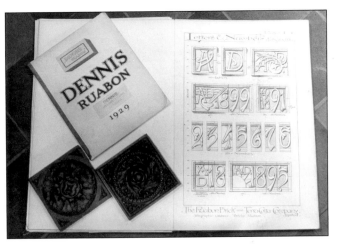

sinking the Legacy Colliery, where he constructed another tramway. Over the next few years he had developed several successful industrial enterprises, and had had dealings with the Ruabon Coal Company. In the same year that his Ruabon Coal and Coke Company took over operations from the Ruabon Coal Company, Henry Dennis also started a tilery in Hafod, the Red Works. Here, bricks were made for Hafod Colliery, but soon it became apparent that brick production had a future in its own right.

By 1893 a purpose-built brickworks had been set up at Hafod, and clay was being quarried near New Hall. A little later, with the company in the charge of Henry Dennis's son Dyke Dennis after his father's death in 1903, a second factory was established at Pant. Brick, roofing tiles and quarry tiles which are extruded products with a rustic appearance and a limited colour range, were produced at Haford, as was terracotta, unglazed clay which is fired at high temperatures and can be moulded into a variety of decorative forms. The new factory manufactured complementary products such as glazed stoneware, pipes, glazed bricks and glazed tessellated and encaustic tiles.

*Above: Promotional catalogues from 1929. **Left:** The hand press team pressing quarry tiles in the 1930s.*

Ruabon brick is bright red, very durable and very distinctive. It was favoured for a long time both for practical and for aesthetic reasons. It is a testimony to its remarkable technical properties that many buildings constructed in Victorian and Edwardian times are still in virtually perfect condition today, and Ruabon brick, because of its durability, is a strong selling point for any house. It became especially sought-after following the Gothic revival around the turn of the century, when decorative brickwork became popular and architects such as Pugin and Waterhouse featured brick in much of their work, setting a trend which was to continue through Edwardian times and after.

Brick production at Hafod became more efficient in 1920 when the Hoffman kiln, which was to remain in use until brick production finally ceased, was built. The following year the factory at Pant was sold, and in 1933 Hafod Colliery, too, was sold. The intervening 12 years had been difficult ones, and the hard times in the industry continued throughout the 30s. A climate of industrial unrest had developed, leading up to the miners' and general strikes. Brick manufacture was labour intensive and sometimes dangerous; the tileries employed up to 450 workers, mainly men, to produce relatively small numbers of bricks and tiles.

The company was reorganised in 1934, the year of the mining disaster which killed 262 miners in an underground explosion in the Dennis section of the Gresford mine; a new private limited company was formed, with its main objectives being the production of bricks, quarry tiles, roofing tiles, fireplaces and chimney pots. The company was called Dennis Ruabon Limited, thus formally adopting the name which had from the beginning been stamped on its bricks, and it continued to prosper, first under Dyke Dennis until his death in 1944, then under his son Patrick Dennis. One of the major costs involved in ceramic production is that of fuel, and Dennis Ruabon recognised that long-term benefits would result from investment in more economical sources of energy. In 1948 a long-term modernisation programme began, which included electrification, mechanical presses and improved coal-fired underfeed stokers for the kilns, and in 1958 the factory switched from coal to oil.

It was arguably the company's commitment to modernisation and investment which assured its future; in 1960 Dennis Ruabon acquired Ruabon Brick and Terracotta, which had been in production since 1883 at the Gardden Works in Johnstown, and around the same time J C Edwards, which had not invested to the same extent as Dennis Ruabon, ceased production. This left Dennis Ruabon the only tile manufacturer in Wales.

*Above: The workforce from the 1930s.*

tions, and the total cost of the investment amounted to £4m. In the meanwhile, the site at Gardden had been sold. The new factory came on stream in the Spring of 1983. At last the company was in a position to meet and exceed the existing demand for quarry tiles, and was able to develop its range of products to exploit the market to the full. In order to make the range of quarry tiles as wide as possible, a new intermittent kiln was installed for short runs of new, relatively low volume products. The company also took this opportunity to diversify into the clay paver market. Although clay pavers are far outsold by concrete pavers for general use, they are technically superior and are therefore preferred for long-term installations such as pedestrian areas. Clay pavers from Hafod can be seen in Taiwan, in Japan - and in Wrexham town centre.

More than 120 years after its foundation by Cornish-born entrepreneur Henry Dennis, the company is still going strong, and during that time it has bequeathed innumerable fine examples of brick and terracotta work to many parts of England and Wales. Besides all the fine buildings constructed of Ruabon brick, their legacy includes ornament to the surfaces of buildings in very high quality terracotta, the lettering on public buildings, and a wide variety of ornamental bricks and panels, mouldings for cornices and elaborate designs for terminals and arches. Having proved that it can adapt both its products and its processes to keep abreast of change, there is no doubt that Dennis Ruabon will continue to meet whatever challenges the future might bring, and the familiar name which has been stamped in brick for over a century will continue to be synonymous with quality, artistry and durability for many generations to come.

There was a high demand, both in the UK and overseas, for the robust Welsh quarry tiles, to the extent that the company found it increasingly difficult to produce them in sufficient quantity. In 1964 the decision was taken to discontinue the production of bricks in order to concentrate exclusively on tile production.

The next two major changes in the company occurred in 1970: Patrick Dennis died and was succeeded by his son Jeremy Dennis, and North Sea Gas replaced oil as fuel. The company was still struggling to meet demand for quarry tiles, and preliminary consideration was given to building a brand new factory at Hafod. By 1978, the year in which the company celebrated its centenary, these plans had been finalised. A new automated tile production factory was to be constructed, with a large tunnel kiln to be supplied by a German manufacturer as no British manufacturer was able to meet the specifica-

**Both pictures:** *Recent examples of the company's fine craftsmanship.*

# Industry in a beautiful environment

Industry came to the Flexsys' site at Cefn Mawr in 1867, when Robert Graesser and Timothy Crowther began extracting oil from shale from the nearby collieries to produce lamp-oil, lubricating oil and paraffin wax. Unfortunately, imported American oil became available more cheaply, so instead they became chemists, with Crowther moving to separate premises nearby. Graesser extracted cresylic acid and phenol from crude tar acids brought from the Midlands by canal barge; phenol was important as an antiseptic, and its derivative, salicylic acid, had pharmaceutical uses. By 1910, the Cefn Mawr Chemical Works was producing more than half the world's supply of phenol. In 1920 the works became the Graesser-Monsanto Chemical Works following a 50 per cent acquisition by Monsanto; Monsanto took over completely eight years later. Production of saccharin commenced, and a plant was built to convert salicylic acid into acetylsalicylic acid - better known as aspirin.

Research into the reaction of phenol with formaldehyde in the 1920s resulted in the development of synthetic resins. Graesser-Monsanto supplied phenol and cresol for the manufacture of the new phenol plastics, whose properties made them ideal insulants for radio and electrical parts.

Production of the rubber chemicals which are produced here today began after 1930. The growth in the rubber tyre market naturally led to increased demand for the chemicals used in their manufacture: accelerators to speed up the vulcanisation process, vulcanisation inhibitors to control the onset of vulcanisation so that the rubber can be shaped before the process starts, and

antidegradants to make tyres last longer. New rubber chemicals were added to the product range during the 1950s and the 1970s. In 1995 the plant became part of a newly-formed international company, Flexsys Rubber Chemicals Ltd. Flexsys is a joint venture between Monsanto (now Solutia) and Akzo Nobel, a Netherlands-based chemicals company.

Ruabon despatches about 25,000 tonnes of chemical products each year, with about 90 per cent being exported to over 70 countries around the world, generating an annual revenue of approximately £60 million for the UK economy. The plant provides direct employment for around 400 people, and the site covers an area of 160 acres. It is located in an area of outstanding natural beauty, close to a national park, and conservation of the environment is a priority; Millions of pounds have been invested over the last decade on a water treatment plant to protect the River Dee, in addition to other significant investments on the operating units and site infrastructure. The company has close links with the community, encouraging feedback on its future plans and taking an active interest in local schools, charities and voluntary organisations. Educational visits from schools and other organisations are welcomed - and an unexpected bonus for first-time visitors is Flexsys' on-site trout hatchery, where trout are reared to stock the various fishing areas on the river Dee!

*Above: An aerial view of the Water Treatment Plant. Left: The site set amidst beautiful countryside.*

# Made in Wrexham - the material with a multitude of uses

Polypropylene must surely be one of the most versatile materials ever invented. It is light-weight but strong, and is resistant to abrasion, to extremes of temperature and to chemicals. So the barrier cladding and kickboards which surround the ice skating rinks at Durham, Whitley Bay and other towns are made of Propylex; the imitation coal effect on Berry Magicoal electric fires is made of Propylex; Nuttall Riley's sweets travel down Propylex chutes and Weetabix flakes pass through Propylex boxes on their way from the rolling mill to the biscuit making department; the Ram Brewery's yeast skimmer is made out of Propylex; pigs are slaughtered in slaughter halls with Propylex-cladded walls; and ice cream is delivered in vans lined with Propylex. The Maxitanks in which Crosse & Blackwell store the ingredients of Branston Pickle are made of Celmar, as are Anglian Water's 25,000 gallon drinking-water storage tank and the four massive towers used for the the treatment of gas given off during the production of phosphoric acid at the Jordan Fertiliser Company Limited, Aqaba. And both Propylex and Celmar, together with other kinds of extruded polypropylene sheet, are made by Royalite Plastics Limited at Wrexham.

Wrexham has been a major site for the manufacture of man-made materials for almost half a century, but it was 30 years before the opening of the synthetic yarn

factory at Wrexham that the market for these products first began to be explored. In the period which followed the First World War, the British Cellulose and Chemical Manufacturing Company at Spondon, which had been set up in 1916 to produce cellulose acetate for use as a non-inflammable coating, or 'dope', for aeroplane wings during the war, began looking for other ways of putting this material to use. Drs Henri and Camille Dreyfus, the scientists who had developed the cellulose acetate material, proposed converting cellulose acetate flakes into artificial fibres.

*Above:* The Celanese Magazine from 1955.
*Below:* A packing table fabricated from Propylex.

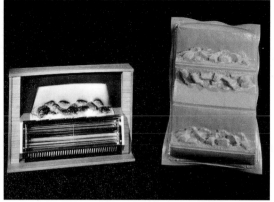

world output of rayon rose from 29 million pounds to over 2,200 million pounds. But besides 'Celanese' fibre, there was also 'Celanese' plastic, which was made by adding plasticisers and other modifying substances to cellulose acetate flake to create a substance which could take the form of either plastic sheet or film. A large quantity of spectacle frames and eye shields were made out of sliced sheet, and uses of film included laminating record covers and books.

After the Second World War, British Celanese drew up ambitious plans to build a new factory for the production of cellulose acetate fibre for clothing. An area of land just outside Wrexham which had been occupied by an immense Royal Ordnance factory during the war became available for private industrial use, and British Celanese leased a site consisting of around 240 acres of semi-derelict land and the buildings which stood on it.

This opened up a tremendous range of possibilities for applications in the plastics and textile fields, and led to the launch of such varied products as the glass-substitute 'Spondite', acetate 'artificial silk' which became known as rayon, a new acetate plastic called 'Celastoid' and various other man-made yarns for weaving and knitting. Having established these new and highly marketable products, the British Cellulose and Chemical Manufacturing Company then held a competition amongst its employees to find a new name for the company which would reflect the direction in which it was moving. Dr Henri Dreyfus suggested 'Celanese', and it was this name which was chosen in 1923, and which subsequently became the household name for the new man-made cellulose acetate fibre which was to become very popular for women's underwear, tights and other items of clothing. Production statistics give a clear indication of the rapid growth of this industry: between 1919 and 1939,

*Above left:* A large spiral chute fabricated from British Celanese Propylex polypropylene sheet.
*Above right:* Propylex imitation coal effects for electric fires.
*Below :* The British Celanese Ltd stand at Interplas 61.

Some of the buildings could be converted to house warp knitting machines, while others were turned into a plastics department, and those that could not be used were demolished. Major construction work began in 1950; the whole site was excavated, new foundations and services were laid, and the main and ancillary factory buildings were connected by bridges, to facilitate the continual, easy flow of products through the various stages of manufacture. The various stages in the building of the new factory are recounted in an article in the company's magazine, which includes the following summary of what was involved: 'RECIPE FOR BUILDING A NEW FACTORY: Take a derelict site - Excavate and remove 378,000 cubic yards of earth - Mix and lay 55,000 cubic yards of concrete - Erect 10,000 tons of steel - Lay 4,500,000 bricks - Season with frayed tempers, hot air and tears of frustration - Baste repeatedly with rainwater - And you have a new factory building. But it's not quite as simple as that.'

This company magazine, entitled 'The Celanese Magazine', was launched at around this time to help the staff keep in touch as the company expanded, and it gives an invaluable insight into life at British Celanese during the mid 1950s. It records such events as the transfer of a number of members of staff from Spondon to Wrexham, the engagement of a young lady employed in the electrical department at Wrexham to Mr K Matthews, the Wrexham FC footballer, and the success of a team from the Wrexham factory in the Chester and District Fire Services Competition. Overall the magazine conveys a very favourable picture of the company, characterised by what the Vice-Chairman and Managing Director, in his message in the first magazine, calls 'the friendly spirit which marks . . . the Celanese family'.

There had been great rivalry, during the early years of the development of man-made fibres, between British Celanese and Courtaulds, each of whom was responsible for significant scientific breakthroughs. British Celanese merged with Courtaulds in 1957, although it continued to use the name British Celanese for a time. During the 1970s the company, now using the name of Courtaulds, worked alongside ICI in the development of the market potential of polypropylene, and this has become the focus of manufacture at Wrexham. In 1990 Courtaulds sold the site to Royalite Plastics, part of British Vita Plc. Royalite is continuing the tradition of innovation which has characterised the company from origins in the first world war, and new applications are constantly being found as research into the behaviour of thermoplastics and the development of new manufacturing techniques continues.

*Above: The white barrier cladding and blue kick board at the Billingham Ice Rink were produced with Propylex. Rinks at Durham and Whitley Bay were similarly supplied.*

# The company whose board has brought success

Kronospan Chirk was established in 1970 by the Kaindl family, who selected the 56 acre site at Wrexham as the site for a chipboard factory because of its excellent road and rail links with all parts of the UK and its proximity to supplies of raw materials. The subsequent growth of the company has proved that their choice of location was perfect. Now occupying well over 100 acres, Kronospan has the capacity to process over a million tonnes of raw material a year. Some 40,000 timber deliveries are received each year, and processed on plant which includes the latest melamine faced chipboard presses, three paper impregnation lines, ContiRoll chipboard and medium density fibreboard lines. The company has a workforce approaching 500, making it one of the area's largest employers, and manufacturing continues around the clock, 365 days a year, to meet demand.

Chipboard production is a complex process, and one where commercial factors must be carefully balanced with environmental considerations. Kronospan's working practices are stringent, using the latest technologies and the highest standard of equipment. With a firm commitment to Waste Minimisation Techniques, the company's re-cycling successes have surpassed all expectations, attaining 100 per cent utilisation of all raw materials.

Timber is the basic raw material used in chipboard manufacture; Kronospan uses timber from properly managed, sustainable supplies, and its 'Forest Friendly' products all carry the FICGB Woodmark in

recognition of this. The company only manufactures products which can be transported, stored and used safely. These products fall into four categories: chipboard, MDF (medium density fibreboard), MFC (melamine faced chipboard) and sawn timber from the on-site sawmill. Kronospan is a supplier to the leading names in the building, timber distribution and furniture manufacturing industries, and almost 20 per cent of all chipboard used in the UK each year, and over 40 per cent of all MDF used, is produced at Kronospan Chirk.

With environmental objectives which far exceed the requirement of the UK Environmental Protection Act, Kronospan's commitment to continuous improvement has earned the award of BS EN ISO9002, and it is working towards World Class Manufacturing and environmental standards. At the heart of its success lies the concept of Progress, a concept shared with the group of companies of which it is a member; founded in 1897 in the mountains of Austria, Kronospan now comprises many factories across Europe, offering products in a wide variety of patterns and finishes, all produced using ecologically and environmentally-sound methods.

*Above: Luxfloor, one of the company's products.*
*Left: The Chirk production site.*

# Talented Architects - Consistent Prizewinners

All around Wrexham, TACP's distinguished contribution to both built and natural environment is in evidence, from restoration work on St Giles Parish Church to Wrexham Maelor Hospital, from the restoration of Erddig Hall and Chirk Castle to the new Yale College of Further Education, and from the Miners Institutes at Rhosllanerchrugog and Llay to the new Sports Centre at NEWI.

TACP stands for The Anthony Clark Partnership, and the foundations for this successful architectural practice were laid in 1906 when F A Roberts established a practice in Mold. His nephew, Fred Roberts, subsequently formed a partnership with H Anthony Clark, Borough Architect for Wrexham Borough Council, and in 1949 the firm of H Anthony Clark, F C Roberts and Partners had offices in both Mold and Wrexham. They were joined in 1950 by Robert Barclay Heaton, who five years later became a Partner in the Wrexham office. In 1956 an association with the Liverpool architectural practice of Spence Atkinson took them into Liverpool, and a new office was opened in Warrington in 1960. The Warrington office, headed by Jack Garstang, handled work for the Atomic Energy Commission but subsequently closed when a change of policy resulted in Atomic Energy projects being undertaken in-house. Also in 1960, Brian Evans, the head of Spence Atkinson in Liverpool, became a Partner.

The Partnership adopted the briefer name of The Anthony Clark Partnership in 1961, a time of growing involvement in numerous commissions for banks, housing and hospitals, including the new Dental Hospital in Liverpool, and one very successful project undertaken around this time was a housing development at Horsemans Green which

resulted in the practice being awarded the the Royal Institute of British Architects Gold Medal for Architecture.

In 1963 Dennis Griffith, who many years earlier had worked with F A Roberts in the Mold office before moving to London, rejoined the firm, becoming a Partner in 1966. A merger with Nelson and Parker in the late 60s brought Joe R Parker into the firm, and he became a Partner in 1974. With the expansion of the Partnership came a move to new premises in Wrexham, where for many years the office had been located above the photographic studio of Mr Algernon Smith in Regent Street. The firm moved from here to its present offices in Grosvenor Road where John Cragg, a local Quantity Surveyor, once lived.

H Anthony Clark retired in 1974 after 25 years with the Partnership; and it was at this stage that the firm's name was simplified to TACP.

*Above: Wrexham Maelor Hospital.*
*Below: Erddig Hall, Wrexham.*

Two noteworthy projects undertaken for The National Trust around this time included the restoration of Erddig Hall, Wrexham, and the restoration of Ice House, Powis Castle; both these received the Prince of Wales Award, in 1977 and 1984 respectively, and Erddig Hall also won the Museum of the Year Award. The practice carried out work on nearly all the National Trust properties in North Wales.

Robert Barclay Heaton's many years' contribution to Welsh Architecture was recognised by being awarded the OBE in 1992.

1984 also saw the opening of TACP's Cardiff office, widening the practice's ability to provide landscape and environmental services throughout the Principality and beyond.

Two years later, the Partnership reformed, under the direction of Dennis Griffith as Senior Partner; the Partnership was now composed of Robert Heaton (son of Robert Barclay Heaton), Brian Jones, David Jones, John Pugh, Gareth West and T Wesley Wright. TACP Design, an associate practice, was established in Liverpool, with TACP continuing to practice from its offices in Wrexham and Cardiff. It now offered a multi-disciplinary range of services for the design and construction industry, employing its own architects, environmental consultants, landscape architects, urban designers, interior designers, building and quantity surveyors. Since this time, the firm has won a steady flow of Design Awards: the BALI National Landscape Civic Trust Award for Land Reclamation/Erosion Control for the Swansea Enterprise Park in 1988; the Snowdonia National Park Award and the Civic Trust Award for the restoration of Ty Mawr, Gwynedd, for The National Trust, in 1989; the BALI National Trust Award for the Parc Tawe Hothouse, Swansea, in 1990 and the Prince of Wales Award for Pennant Melangell, Powys, in 1992; and in 1996 it won the Civic Trust Award for Tenby Harbour and Environs, the National Care Home Design Award and Civic Society Award for the Nightingale Hospice, Wrexham, the Lord Mayor's Civic Award and the Cardiff 2000 Environment Award for Britannia Park. Civic Society Awards were also won in 1996 for Phase 1 of Yale College, and in

1998 for Gwilym Hughes and Partners Solicitors offices, Wrexham Museum and further developments at Yale College. It is a rare year that TACP does not win a Civic Society Award!

When, after a long association with the Partnership, Dennis Griffith retired in 1993, Gareth West became Senior Partner. Hilary Morgan, a landscape architect, became a Partner in 1993.

Today, the practice offers a comprehensive and integrated consultancy service covering all the needs of the construction industry, and its current staff of more than 40 professional architects, designers and surveyors continues to provide a complete range of professional design, planning and management skills to carry any project through each stage to a successful - and potentially award-winning - conclusion.

*Above: The Miner's Institute.*
*Top: Yale College of Further Education.*

# The company that began in striking circumstances . . .

The General Strike of 1926 brought widespread disruption to the country, and few companies which were in business then look back at this time with much satisfaction. But one company which might well remember the General Strike with a degree of affection, and indeed which might not even exist today had it not been for the strike, is J H Willis Ltd. Before the strike, dairy farmer John Everard Willis had relied on the railway to transport the milk produced on his farm Cam'yr'Alyn, in Rossett; each day their milk was loaded onto the farm lorry and Mr Willis' son, John Harold Willis, would drive it to Rossett station and put it on the train. But one day no train came, because the railway unions had called their members out on strike. So, not wanting to waste the whole consignment, and being a resourceful kind of chap, Harold Willis solved the

*Above: One of the company's earlier methods of transport. Above left: John Harold Willis, founder of the company. Below: A newer version of their transportation fleet.*

bombs exploding all around; as long as the road was clear, the lorry would keep going. Sometimes the explosions were so close that lumps of flying masonry would hit the lorry, and it was not unusual to find bits of masonry in the churns at the end of a bad night run. At the depot, which now housed a searchlight, constant vigilance was needed; the lorries could not be left in the open because of reflection from the churns, so they had to be parked under trees all the time.

problem by simply driving the milk directly to Liverpool Co-op on the back of the farm lorry. In this way Cam'yr'Alyn was able to continue producing and distributing milk throughout the strike, and the method of transport which they had tried as an emergency measure proved so efficient that when the strike finished, they decided to carry on taking their milk to Liverpool themselves. Other dairy farmers began to show an interest, and Harold Willis agreed to transport their milk along with his father's. He realised that there was a future in what he was doing, and began to look into the possibility of buying his own lorry. With a loan from his mother, he bought an REO Speedwagon, and his investment paid off. Soon he needed a second lorry which was driven by Dennis Dunning.

By the late 1930s a fleet of six vehicles was collecting milk from farms in Cheshire, Denbighshire and Flintshire, and was also transporting Ministry of Food milk (secondary milk) to Liverpool and Staffordshire. Nineteen thirty-five saw the formation of the Milk Marketing Board; arrangements for milk distribution were formalised, and the MMB contracted J H Willis to carry ex-farm milk to Liverpool, as they had been doing for some time, and also to carry secondary milk on behalf of Cadbury's, Bangor on Dee.

At the beginning of the war, the company had acquired their first diesel lorry, but this was requisitioned when war broke out and a petrol Bedford was purchased instead. During the war years, J H Willis continued transporting milk under difficult and dangerous conditions. Rossett had the misfortune to be on the bomb run to Liverpool. Journeys to Liverpool were made twice a day, often with

Having survived the war, business prospered and J H Willis' fleet kept on growing; by the 1950s the fleet comprised 12 vehicles, which included both tankers for the secondary milk and churn wagons for the ex-farm milk. In the 1970s, by which time milk was no longer transported in churns, the fleet had increased to 24 secondary tankers and six ex-farm tankers. In 1989 the MMB carried out a rationalisation programme designed to improve the efficiency of ex-farm transportation, and under the new arrangements J H Willis Ltd administered the 14-tanker fleet of Willmorr Haulage as well as its own 27 secondary tankers.

Willmorr Haulage was closed down in November 1994, and J H Willis Ltd returned to farm collection. Now located at Gresford Bank, the company currently operates 28 secondary tankers with a capacity of 25,000 litres each, and 22 ex-farm tankers. These vehicles deliver milk throughout the UK, excluding only Scotland and the south east, and because most dairy companies use J H Willis's service, the company is able to combine delivery for different companies in its schedule for the same day. J H Willis has also, along the way, become the owner of a tyre company. Altogether it has 62 employees on the payroll, of whom seven can boast over 25 years' service. Dennis Dunning's two sons still work for the company, and it is owned by Robert and Ruth Willis.

*Above: Another lorry owned by the company.*

# Practice made perfect

The firm of Allington Hughes has been in Wrexham since 1826 when Thomas Hughes, a young Solicitor from St Asaph, set up his practice. This probably makes it the oldest firm of solicitors in Wrexham. In due course his eldest son, John Allington Hughes joined him. After his father's death John carried on the practice until his retirement in 1903 when Joseph Henry Bate, who had become a partner in 1899, succeeded him. Joseph was joined for a while by Cyril Newman, but by the time of his death in 1932 Cyril had left Wrexham and it was Joseph's son, John Allington Warburton Bate, who inherited the practice. Apart from a period during the Second World War when he served with the Welsh Guards, John ran the firm until his retirement in 1970.

The firm was then taken over by James C R Bowden, who had a long standing connection with Allington, Hughes & Bate. In 1971 Paul F Craddock, who had served his Articles of Clerkship with John A W Bate, became a partner.

John A Partington, who had also served his Articles with the firm, became a partner in 1984. Two years later Allington Hughes & Bate amalgamated with David Hughes & Co of Chester and Wrexham, and became Allington Hughes Solicitors.

The enlarged firm at Wrexham then included the Wrexham partners (Christopher M J Williams and David N H Parry) of David Hughes & Co who practised from Midland Bank Chambers at that time. In 1988 T Vincent Ryan became a partner, followed by Melissa Haycock in 1997 and Gavin Rogers in 1998.

During the 170 plus years which it has been in practice, Allington Hughes has changed premises in Wrexham several times. During the 1850s the firm occupied 31/32 Regent Street but just before the turn of the century moved to 4 Regent Street. In 1975 it relocated to 11 Grosvenor Road, staying there for 12 years. Finally it moved across the road to 10 Grosvenor Road, a fine Victorian building which had just been refurbished.

The firm is committed to serving the community; it was one of the first law firms in the Country to receive a franchise from the Legal Aid Board. It also serves a wide range of businesses in the local area.

The name of Allington Hughes has become familiar to Wrexham people not only by virtue of its legal services but also because the firm is very much involved in community activities such as the sponsorship of musical events.

With over forty staff and ten partners Allington Hughes has the expertise to serve the local community for years to come.

*Above: A recent advertisement of Allington Hughes.*
*Below: Nine of the partners of Allington Hughes in 1998.*

# Precision processes customised for customers by Rexam of Wrexham

Although Rexam Coated Films and Papers has occupied its present site on the Wrexham Industrial Estate for 30 years, many local people who see the factory every day remember the name because of its co-incidental resemblance to Wrexham, but still have no very clear idea of what Rexam actually *do*. And yet many of these people, along with millions throughout the world who have never even heard of Rexam, actually use its products every day, as among other things Rexam is the world leader in paint film technology for vehicles, and a major supplier to the instant photography market.

Rexam is part of Rexam PLC, which is a global organisation with its headquarters in London. Rexam PLC has more than 150 manufacturing sites worldwide, focused on various businesses including building and engineering, industrial packaging, food and beverage packaging, healthcare packaging, beauty packaging, printing, and coated films and papers. Rexam at Wrexham is part of the Coated Films and Papers sector, whose mission is to provide the very best precision coating and laminating. This is a very specialised area, though paradoxically it has a wide range of applications, including for example dielectric films and flexible circuit laminates for the electronics industry; printing plates and hard coat films for graphic artists; photosensitive and imagesetting films for use in imaging; and wound dressing component films for medical use. Precision is important; coatings are manufactured to very strict tolerances using equipment specially designed and manufactured for Rexam which is then modified using proprietary techniques. Customers include leading international companies who find that using the services of Rexam is advantageous to them in terms of efficiency and cost-effectiveness, bringing them all the benefits of the purchasing power and the latest research development to which Rexam, as part of Rexam PLC, is privy, as well as avoiding the need for huge capital investment and the costs of employing and training specialist staff.

Inside the Wrexham factory, the sophisticated, high-tech equipment includes a pilot/development line able to coat flexible materials up to 54 inches wide and enabling adjustments to be made on-line with more than 50 variables being monitored and logged by computer. The workforce consists of around 150 employees, some of whom can boast over 20 years service, having started working there when the factory first opened. During this period they have seen a continual programme of technological improvements and the introduction of new speciality products, and there is no doubt that this trend will continue . . . so keeping up to date with exactly what Rexam *do* will never be easy!

*Above: The Rexam building in 1984...*
**Left:** *...and today.*

# A moving story

Moving house, as most people discover sooner or later, can be a stressful experience; but the people of Wrexham are fortunate because, whatever other worries they have, they need never worry about the actual removal. They know that at the appointed time a big, red van will draw up outside, and an experienced team will take charge of carefully transferring their household contents to their new home. It would be safe to estimate that at least 90 per cent of Wrexham families have, on at least one occasion, entrusted their treasured possessions to one of these big, red vans - and the name on the side? - Thomas Transport, of course!

Thomas Transport was established as a removals business by Gordon Thomas in 1920. The firm's first vehicles were horse-drawn, and they operated from the Old Brewery on Salop Road. Gordon Thomas was, in due course, joined in the business by his son Herbert, and over the years the business evolved; horse-drawn vehicles were replaced by motorised transport, and the company's activities were extended to include general haulage as well as domestic removals. Thomas's investment in motorised transport received an unexpected setback, however, when war broke out and their vehicles were requisitioned for Army use. But that was by no means the worst surprise that the war had in

store for the family: Herbert was captured and held in Japan as a prisoner of war for some considerable time. Happily he was released unhurt to return to the family concern. By this time the company had moved to Caia Road, and shortly after the end of the war they moved again to their current premises at 50 Salop Road. After the war the business grew rapidly; the local coal mines were in full production and needed reliable transport, and Thomas, always alert to the needs of the surrounding area, expanded their operations to oblige. This did not mean that they no longer carried out domestic removals; helping the people of Wrexham to move house remained as important a part of the business as ever, and by now many of their customers were the younger generation of the families who had used their services in the company's early days.

For a while, Thomas Transport was the largest privately owned haulage company in North Wales, but as the coal industry declined Thomas began to undertake more general haulage, specialising at one stage in transporting abnormal loads, whilst domestic removals remained, as ever, the backbone of the business.

Today, removals are still the primary focus of Thomas' business, with containerised storage playing an increasingly important role. The transport fleet consists of four removal vans and eight haulage vehicles with trailers, and their staff currently numbers 15, although it is a standing joke in Wrexham that everyone who holds a Class I licence has worked for Thomas at one time or another! With approximately 15,000 square feet of specialised warehousing space at their disposal, they have ample room for containerised storage, and future plans for the business include placing more emphasis on furniture containerised facilities. They also specialise in cable carrying, for BICC, for which stepframe trailers (semi low loaders) are used, with a lorry-mounted crane to lift the drums of cable on and off. Another specialised service which they offer is commercial archiving for local companies, which involves supplying companies with archive boxes for documents which are then removed stored in crates at Thomas's premises for seven years, during which time they can be accessed as required.

Thomas Transport is a forward-looking company, and their success is due in no small part to their willingness to respond to the needs of their customers, and to take advantage of every new opportunity to enhance the service they offer. The company is on the Internet, and it is not unusual for them to be called upon to arrange shipment of cargos to the other side of the world. But their main strength lies in their commitment to the traditional values, which successive generations of Wrexham families have come to depend on over the years, and which has been in no way affected by their excursions into new spheres - or indeed by their brush with Royalty: Thomas were responsible for Princess Di's butler's removal out of Kensington Palace! For over 70 years the company has built up its reputation for reliable and courteous service to local residents, and they are justly proud of this reputation. There is nothing more rewarding than to be told by customers who ring up to book a big, red van that they have chosen Thomas Transport "because my family always uses you". By continuing to deliver the same exemplary service, Thomas intends to ensure that this compliment is repeated by generations yet to be born.

*Above: Gordon Thomas, founder of the company.*
*Left: The fleet in the 1950s.*

# The company whose founder had to stop making bread to make dough

Arthur Cartwright was a baker by trade. But during the war, supplies of flour ran low, and he had to find other ways of making a living. In 1946 two of his friends came out of the army and set up in business making fireplaces. The two men were Mr Roberts and Mr Evans, and they called their business R & E Fireplaces. However, although they were good craftsmen, they were not such good salesmen, and they were fortunate that Arthur Cartwright was able to help them sell their wares. Before long it was arranged that Arthur should join them as an equal partner, and the firm then became R E C Fireplaces.

This was the beginning of a succession of fireplace ventures for Arthur. In 1948 he started his own business at Kent Road in Brymbo. Another fireplace manufac-turer called Hampton & Lee went into receivership and was purchased in 1951 by Mr Jimmy Finch of Pendyn Hall, but when Mr Finch unfortunately suffered a stroke he sold the premises and business to Arthur Cartwright. Arthur transferred the business to the Old Fan House on Top Road, in Summerhill, where he finally settled, running the business from there until his premature death in 1967.

Arthur's business at Brymbo was called Kent Tiled Fireplaces, and one of the lads he employed to work for him was Henry Gould, usually known as Harry. After Arthur's death, Kent Tiled Fireplaces, which was a thriving concern with a dozen or so employees building and delivering fireplaces, passed to his widow, Mrs Anne Cartwright, and on 2nd February 1968 she sold the business to Harry Gould.

Harry made it into a limited company with himself as principal shareholder and his wife, Betty, as Company Secretary and Director. In spite of initial cashflow problems he kept on the 12 employees, who in return, as a

*Above left:* Arthur Cartwright, founder of the company.
*Below:* The company's Oswestry site in a picture dating from the late 1970s.

Road, Gwersyllt holds some 5,000 items of stock at any one time, and the firm will supply everything needed for house building; it can also meet the specifications of architects and other clients, ordering rare and specialised items from the specialised manufacturers with whom they have contacts and importing quality tiles and terracotta products from Spain and Portugal.

gesture of support to their new boss, volunteered to work for nothing on Saturday mornings for the first 12 months. This was a gesture which Harry never forgot. All 12 employees have remained with him throughout their working lives, leaving only when the time comes to retire.

In 1970 the business moved into purpose-built premises on a former coal tip site which Harry had purchased in Gwersyllt. By this time gas and electricity had begun to take over from solid fuel as methods of heating, and an increasing number of homes were switching over to central heating. As fireplaces went out of fashion, Harry began to diversify into kitchens and bathrooms, which were sold to clients over a 50-mile radius under the trade name of Celtic Kitchens, and building supplies. The name of the company was later changed to Kent Supplies Ltd to reflect the change of focus, although even today the company still produces a small number of fireplaces, which are built by one of Harry's original employees.

The company celebrated its 30th anniversary at Wrexham in February 1998, and the list of suppliers who joined in offering their congratulation tells its own tale, including as it does many of Britain's best-known manufacturers of quality and specialist building materials. Kent Supplies' premises in Mold

THE COMPANY CELEBRATED THIRTY YEARS IN WREXHAM IN FEBRUARY 1998

Another depot was opened in 1975 in Oswestry. Between them, the two branches employ a total staff of 38, many of whom have worked for the company for a very long time indeed; Harry kept up the old tradition of presenting employees with a gold watch to commemorate 25 years service, and at the time of writing over a fifth of the workforce had earned their long-service awards. Amongst the company's long-standing employees are two of Harry's nephews; and his three children, sons Paul and Stephen and daughter Sarah, are directors of the company. The last member of the Cartwright family to work for Kent Supplies retired in 1997 at the age of 65, but still maintains close links with the company.

Harry's own role in the business is now that of consultant, as he passes on to the next generation of Goulds the experience that Arthur Cartwright passed on to him. Built as it is on a firm foundation of employee loyalty, family commitment and traditional values and respected by clients and suppliers alike, Kent Supplies Ltd can look forward to a successful future, bringing the very best range of building materials to customers old and new.

*Above: The Wrexham branch in the 1980s.*

*Celebrations during the Queen's Coronation Tour of 1953*

# Acknowledgments

*Women's Royal Voluntary Service - Welsh Division*
*Wrexham Archives & Museum Services, Wrexham County Borough Council*

*Thanks are also due to:*
*Bob Gray and Helen Gwerfyl, who both assisted with the research for the editorial*
*Peggy Burns who penned the editorial text and*
*Margaret Wakefield for her copywriting skills*